Reiki Rays

Journey

of a Blind Man

Phillip Hawkins

Reiki Master Teacher Trainer Assessor

Copyright

Front cover design by: Barry Hamilton

For my wife Denise

My love, my life and inspiration.

*My strength and courage in those moments when
my own deserts me.*

Work by The Same Author

Reiki: Hold my beer, I've got this

Reiki: One student to another

The Kid who couldn't fit in

Better to be freed by the truth than held captive by a lie

Pink is the new Black: When an old hurt becomes a new healing

Psychic Development: Reflections on a theme #4

Psychic Development: Reflections on a theme #3

Wisdom of the Ancients: Reflections on a theme #2

Reiki: Reflections on a theme #1

Table of Contents

You may have perfect vision but still be blind to those things
you refuse to see and accept about yourself.

12

The path of learning must deliver us to our own darkness
for this is where the greatest teacher patiently awaits our return

Introduction

<hr />

You may have perfect vision but still be blind to those
things you refuse to see and accept about yourself.

Journey of a blind man

<hr />

There are three things that help define the quality of the
life we experience. What we focus on, what it means to us and
what we choose to do about it. Through the power of energy
following intention our thoughts create a blueprint. Our beliefs
are the architect that designs the image and our actions build the

reality we have no option but to live with. If we are unhappy with the choices we make then we must change our decision making process, if we want something different we must do things differently. If not habit and routine will simply refill your standing order you have set in place with the universe.

The process is easier to accept than practice, but its formula is simplicity itself. The quality of life is improved through the quality of your thoughts. This will then have a knock on effect and improve the quality of your beliefs which provides the motivation of your actions in the form of your life choices. Thought, belief and action is the creative formula and we are constantly using it to create the life we lead. Change in life is inevitable; permanency is an illusion with everything in a constant state of flux. Expansion and contraction, growth and decay are an expression of life's cycle of birth, death and rebirth. Each has its own time and place in nature's great scheme of things and when we can live in harmony with this creative flow of energy we will instinctively begin to improve our health and wellbeing. Proactive personal development requires choices to be made which in turn requires alternatives to be available for us to exercise our free will. Before we can do this we must first be aware of the possibilities available to us. Once you accept change is possible and you have the ability to make those life defining changes a reality, you are up and running, even if it's very slowly, one small step at a time.

Belief in your own ability can be a blessing or a curse. It can free you to release your untapped potential and achieve great success, or it can cripple and immobilise you through ignorance and fear, feeling trapped and powerless. A belief no matter how powerful it may appear is nothing more than a feeling of certainty. Often, a belief we have been given, and accepted as our own, on closer inspection is found to be untrue based on lies, misconceptions or family traditions. We believed what our parents told us and accepted it as gospel until we learned to question those traditional family values and truths. Unfortunately our ''teachers'' can only teach what they have learnt themselves and over time traditional beliefs become rigid and set in stone incapable of change and development. What was what is and what shall be must remain the same, unchanged and unchallenged regardless of facts or evidence to the contrary. When faced with an illusion no matter how convincing a dose of reality is the only antidote that is proven to work.

The solution to a problem requires acceptance the problem exists, you can't fix anything until you take the time to discover why it isn't working properly, but thankfully every problem contains the seeds to its own solution. When the problem is closer to home you will need to get to know yourself to figure out what you need to do to repair the damage and achieve optimum health and wellbeing. Unfortunately for you there is a stranger living your life. A stranger who is both friend and ally once you take the time to get to know them and discover what makes them tick. All relationships need to be worked at and the relationship we have with ourselves is often the most neglected. As long as we look to others to sort out our life for us we dis-empower ourselves by adopting a victim mentality; it's our life and we have both duty of care and responsibility to live it. Once we reach this point of self realisation it signals the start of a journey of personal discovery that is both empowering and enlightening as we begin to work through the darkness created by our ignorance and fears.

Chapter One

———◆♦◆———

Our journey to find the great Oz and Wikipedia

———◆♦◆———

Unlike toasters life offers no guarantees. We come into this world with nothing more than our first and last breath and an indeterminate time between to make our journey. Lacking maps, apps and Sat-Nav to help us find our way, the mythical yellow brick road of enlightenment is often no more than crazy paving made up as we go along, struggling as we do to find the Wizards of Oz and Wikipedia with answers to our questions, and solutions to all of our problems.

The path to understanding is very rarely paved with gold, with insufficient light to help us find our way. More often than not, it's a journey of hardship and compromise, a path forged out of necessity and made possible by the unsure faltering steps we are willing or forced to take. It's a journey of self discovery that provides us with the answers we seek. Those who believe in the one true way face disappointment on discovering faith in anything less than truth, knowledge and understanding, lead to dead ends and disillusionment. We must find our own way breaking new ground and old beliefs in the process. Experiences we draw to ourselves and the lessons they contain will like footprints in the sand disappear with our passing. We are all blind to those things we refuse to face and see. We look no further than what we hold to be true and comfort us. Yet what we believe about ourselves is no more than a feeling of certainty based on life's experiences and the truths created by others and accepted as our own.

As we struggle to escape from the darkness of ignorance our vision is often obscured by fear and uncertainties reflected back to us by our unrealistic expectations of life. True knowledge and understanding asks us to release our grip on reality and let go of those beliefs once we have outgrown them. Our momentary point of view is never our final destination. It's no more than a snapshot on a journey to discover who we really are, what we see and hold to be true at any given moment in time is determined by how far we have travelled and the progress we have made. What we see and how we view the scenery around us will change as our perception expends and the universe responds to our growing level of awareness.

You can't trace steps that haven't yet been taken or plot your progress in advance. Its only when I take a moment to look back, I see how far I have travelled on my journey of self discovery from a childhood of abuse neglect and poverty to the realisation of my dreams to be a teacher and writer. My past no matter how traumatic is no more than a point of reference for my destiny will always lie before me; misplaced guilt and regret will only serve as an anchor to my past and stop me moving forward. The biggest challenge I face is accepting how far I have come, and finding the courage to continue my journey and follow where my dreams and aspirations may lead.

All of our experiences are created by the choices we make either consciously or by default, and a lack of understanding or an unwillingness to accept these influences will not release us from their control and the consequences of our actions. Few of us are blessed with the clarity of sight that allows us to see beyond our own fears and uncertainties, our sphere of perception. Even those with 20/20 vision are still capable of tripping over their own doubts and fears, for every experience we create and live through reflects back to us our beliefs and expectations of life. Yet every challenge and new experience presents us with the opportunity to go beyond what we already know about ourselves, break new ground and old beliefs to discover what we are capable of. Change is uncomfortable but personal development always lies beyond the barriers and limitations we set ourselves.

This book chronicles certain life changing events that helped shape the person I have become; crucial moments in time that continue to motivate and empower my development as a person. Reflecting on challenges to be endured and overcome before I could begin to understand who I was and the direction my life was taking. I had no way of knowing at the time, it was a journey that would give me both meaning and a sense of purpose. In the process I stopped looking for someone to blame for the mess my life was in. I started to look for answers, to search for knowledge and understanding and through that process discovered truth can be found hidden in the ashes of old beliefs and fears.

Travel with me for a short while and together we can reflect on some of the hardships and challenges I overcame and the effect they had on me physically, mentally and emotionally. The journey is sign posted by the use of early pieces of work in the form of an 'aid memoire' and to show how a change in my beliefs, my thought processes and ability changed the course of my life forever.

The book *Journey of a Blind Man* reflects my belief that no matter how educated, intelligent qualified or experienced we may be we are blind to the things we do not wish to see or accept about ourselves. As such we are all students on a journey of personal discovery. We have enrolled into this school of life, a journey of discovery carrying the debilitating baggage of self doubt, fear, and uncertainty, struggling with the weight of this burden we stumble from one experience to another trying to find our way. This book began life as an idea; it was sustained by the belief it's both relevant and worthwhile. Driven by the fact the essence of this work has already changed and improved the quality of life for so many people over the last seventeen years and continues to do so. As a journal it's incomplete because our personal journey is a never ending story in which we play many roles; hero and villain, visionary and fool. All travelling together sometimes lost in a wilderness of uncertainty, at other times certain of our direction and purpose.

Each chapter of our life journey provides us with new experiences, a blank page upon which we can leave our mark as testimony to our passing. I'm a blind man trying to make my way through life, sometimes sure of where I'm going but more often than not jumping from one experience to another and hoping for the best. My blindness is not a physical disability, rather it's the blindness of ignorance and fear, and as the old adage says *'In the absence of light darkness prevails'*. Put another way *'In the absence of knowledge and understanding illness, ignorance and fear will take charge'*. I'm ignorant of those things that exert the greatest control over my life. Those deep seated fears and negative beliefs; enemies that lie in wait ready to ambush me and sabotage my efforts the moment I dare to deviate from the path set for me by others so many years ago. This is the story of how Reiki helped me find my own path in life breaking new ground and old beliefs in the process and helped me discover who I was, who I am and the person I hope to become.

The wayward Pilgrim

I am a wayward pilgrim on a journey to who knows where. Lacking a destination, I'm forever looking back seeking reassurance from my own footsteps. Stumbling over my own doubts and fears which seem to lay in wait ready to cause me to stumble and fall. Like a beast of burden, I'm weary and laden down with baggage collected along the way, old and outgrown yet unable to set it down. Fear and uncertainty are my constant companions their voices loud at every turn and mockingly silent at every stop. Overwhelmed by the confusion of my own vulnerability, I look to others to give direction and purpose. Each faltering step takes me unknowingly closer to a destination forever out of reach.

Lost and alone I utter words of despair and seek a moment's peace to collect my troubled thoughts from the darkness and confusion that surrounds me.

In answer to my prayer comes the realisation all the hardships that have befallen me have helped bring me to this point and place of reconciliation and learning. My suffering was always in response to my own resistance, the more I struggled the lower I sank into my fear and despair, and the more painful the experience became. The road is laid bare before me but it's my thoughts and beliefs that create the landscape I call life.

When I stumbled and fell, it was because I had forced myself beyond the point of no return and ignored the voice of reason. I had forgotten that there is a time for all things. There is a time to journey but also a time to rest and wait; a time for reflection on how far I have travelled. It's only when I looked back can I see how far I have come and the progress made. The prodigal son returning home from a journey of self-discovery, to rediscover my spiritual birthright, each step providing me with the experiences necessary to discover who I am. It's the journey within that provides the opportunity to learn, and the moment we look within for the answers we seek, we have begun our journey home.

Chapter Two

A road less travelled is often dimly lit

This book is nothing more than a chapter in my life charting my early faltering steps from a childhood of deprivation and abuse up to a point in time when thanks to a growing dependency on drink and prescribed medication my life imploded and nearly came to a premature end as I tried to commit suicide. Although I didn't realise it at the time, this catastrophic event brought me to a major crossroads in my young life and found me standing outside of a psychiatric hospital. I was shaking with the fear of what the future may hold. I knew instinctively if I walked away I would fall into a dark abyss of mental illness that claimed my mother's life and would inevitably take mine. At that moment in time there was no way of knowing my childhood experiences would play a defining role in my development as a Reiki teacher and writer, and help me find inner peace, purpose and meaning in life.

My beliefs and experiences may not be shared by every reader nor would I expect them to be, and it has to be said from the outset personal hardship is not a prerequisite to personal development or becoming a Reiki practitioner or teacher. Our journey is a personal one and we can do no more than play the cards we draw. Even if you choose to disregard Reiki and challenge its role as my catalyst for change, you will not be able to ignore the transition taking place as each page and chapter of this book leads to an ever changing point of view. Regardless of ability we all have a personal best within us. I believe we all possess a reservoir of innate wisdom that is both genetic and collective as a species; which helped me face and overcome the challenge of writing this book.

I wanted to write it in such a way that's easy to understand. A way of helping you remember your own life purpose and connect to the wisdom of your ancestors and recognise the beliefs formed by your conditioning that lay hidden by your ignorance and fear. One of the greatest barriers to communication is the words we use and the understanding of their true meaning. The simplest point can be lost in the multitude of words we use to explain it. You already have the knowledge you are searching for; what you lack is the understanding and the wisdom to apply that knowledge in your life. In trying to be something we believe we are not, we overlook the opportunity to discover our true self and express our true worth. In helping you to recognise this fact, I will be one step closer to living my own truth.

If we accept that all understanding lies within us, then we must also accept that searching for it in books and earth while teachers may be based on the limiting belief the answers we search for out there somewhere. We believe we are incomplete until we find the holy grail of wisdom, knowledge and understanding. Yes we require teachers, trainers and mentors to awaken the student to their own innate ability and power. To make real progress the student must take responsibility for their own learning. Spoon feeding them with information makes them lazy, dis-empowers them, and creates a victim mentality. Knowledge alone is nothing more information and data. Understanding is when the information becomes meaningful; wisdom is when we apply knowledge and understanding to improve our health and wellbeing.

If we believe our journey of self discovery must take a set length of time, a certain direction accompanied by the obligatory baggage of 'must do's', guilt and fear weighing us down, this belief merely delays our arrival at our destination. Enlightenment and self mastery are innate; we are born with our reservation already booked, but our ticket is open ended allowing the power of our free will to decide how and when we want to arrive. We all make it back to our spiritual home, but we have the final say as to how long the journey will take and the number of comfort breaks we take along the way. Education brings with it a voice and a desire to be heard, it asks us to loosen our grip on the old and established reality, embracing the new and the unknown. As you discover your true self you will come to know the truth, and the truth will set you free.

A *journey of a single step*

There is nothing new under the sun; the more things change the more they stay the same. New inventions are merely forgotten wisdom waiting to be rediscovered by those with minds open enough to receive this knowledge and understanding. Development is a process that builds upon what has gone before and our progress is defined by our willingness to learn and accept how little we know. In doing so we create the opportunity for knowledge and understanding to unfold.

No matter how far we travel our journey is that of a single step that takes us ever forward along the path of our choosing. A journey of both departure and destination; one gives meaning and the other gives a direction and a sense of purpose, but it's each step on that journey which provides us with the experiences that contain the seeds for personal growth and development.

In a haste to reach our destination we overlook the value of a journey that provides us with the opportunity to learn so much, and our destination can appear empty by comparison. Our arrival is always in the present moment; the here and now and the lessons contained when learnt will define our ultimate destination.

Knowledge, understanding and wisdom are born out of the stillness of creation, the wellspring from which all things are formed through an expression of unconditional love. It neither condones nor judges but simply reflects back to us the value we place upon ourselves and the decisions we make.

It never punishes for there is no need, we are our own judge, jury and executioner when life choices create illnesses and dis-ease. We are never punished for our actions but as a result of our actions for we must accept the consequences of the choices we make, be they good or bad.

Each step draws us ever closer to the point where free will is no longer an issue and we have only the desire to reflect the unconditional love that gives us spiritual life everlasting.

Chapter Three

Where my darkness began

My grandfather Nathan Brown or 'Nat' as he was known all of his adult life was born in 1883, the son of a pitman. Very little is known about his early life other than his father, my great grandfather was a hard-working miner who made a meagre living in one of the twenty or so pits and drift mines that littered the region at the time. It's fair to assume that my grandfather's childhood was no different to that of any other at that time, raised in a poor working class family when the average miners wage was £65.00 for a year's work. It's hard to imagine what life was like back then for a child growing up in a small rural community where everyone knew everyone else's business and they all shared the same level of hardship and deprivation. Luxuries were nonexistent and an attitude of make do and mend prevalent in all of the households, a life of hardship created hard people where only the strong would survive.

In 1800's rural England especially in small pit villages the most common form of transport for people was walking or 'shank's pony' as it was known. If you needed to get anywhere you walked or if you were lucky enough you caught a lift on a passing horse and cart. To see a horse drawn cart coming down the street would be a common sight that wouldn't draw undue attention or be a cause for concern. People went about their daily routine that is, until an accident happened that would change and affect the lives of so many people.

The accident happened sometime in 1886 when Nat was just three years old. Although the exact details of what happened have been lost with time, the consequences of that day 131 years ago are as real today as it was then.

A horse drawn cart was making its way down the main street in the village, people were going about their everyday business and children were playing in the street. One of those children was my grandfather and in an unguarded moment he fell under the wheels of the cart crushing his skull. It doesn't take much imagination to visualise the pain and anger of that moment. The tears and screams of anguish, the prayers and promises if only he would be made well again. Had his mother known what the future would hold, she may have listened to the doctor who attended to his wounds and allowed him to die. The doctor informed my great grandmother to accept and prepare for the inevitable death of her son who, in his opinion had no chance of surviving given the extent of his horrific wounds.

The wheel of the cart had literally opened up his skull from the crown to the frontal lobe stopping above his left eye socket. The doctor's prognosis was that he couldn't be saved and that if by some miracle he did survive, the damage was such he would be little more than a vegetable the rest of his life. The doctor was wrong in some ways; he didn't die nor did he spend his life in a vegetative stupor, but he was right about the detrimental effects of the extensive brain damage. In my grandfathers case the damage was so severe he developed many of the symptoms of severe traumatic brain injury, and a violent personality disorder. There are no medical records to draw upon but the stories of my grandfather's violent outbursts and sadistic bullying were told and retold until they became stuff of perverse legend, and in my mother's case something to be proud of and aspire to. What is certain is that from an early age violence became an integral part of my grandfather's emotional and psychological makeup and in his mind a legitimate way of dealing with any situation he found himself in.

The injury he suffered as a small child can be used to explain some or most of his violent aggression, but on numerous occasions throughout his life he demonstrated an almost sly predatory cunning in creating situations whereby friendly socialising would ultimately provide him with the opportunity to beat someone senseless. He would invite strangers he met in the pub back to his home to have a bite to eat. When they had eaten, he would take out a pair of boxing gloves and the unwitting guest would have to fight for their supper. Invariably he would be beaten senseless in the process.

Whilst he appears to have been driven to violence with little or no provocation, age or gender provided no protection. He was no respecter of women and had no hesitation in beating women regardless of age or status with the ferocity and anger he would any man. My mother recounted how my great grandmother a tiny lady, was brutally beaten on a regular basis to such an extent that she would have to sit with leeches on her face to draw off the blood reducing the swelling sufficiently enough to be able to open her eyes to see.

As soon as he could my grandfather took up boxing as a legitimate outlet for his violent nature and because he enjoyed it he was as proficient inside the ring as he was out of it. This coupled with his hard strenuous work in the pits he developed into a big strong powerful man. Maybe it was his size coupled with his violent nature that meant those around him either too scare or just physically incapable to stop him. Either way unchecked he was out of control and in many ways became a law unto himself. Crook was in those days a quiet market town with its weekly market taking place in the centre of the town where local traders would set up their stalls to sell their wares. They must have dreaded the sight of my grandfather walking around the stalls for if he saw something he wanted but didn't have the money he would simply help himself and no one dared do anything to stop him. He eventually paid, but only when it suited him to do so. Even the local police avoided him and would never dream of tackling him one to one. On the numerous occasions he was arrested and hauled in front of the justice of the peace, the police knew he would never go quietly and they would have a fight on their hands, and take several officers with truncheons to beat him into submission. Growing up I heard many stories about my grandfather's fighting prowess, some were obviously fanciful and while some of the stories were amusing; it doesn't take long before the darker side of his complex personality begins to surface.

He thought nothing of using intimidation to take what he wanted, or to get his own way, and when the mood and the madness took him he could raise that violence literally to a different level. One day he was having a heated argument with someone close to a railway bridge. On hearing the train approaching he dragged the man to the bridge and threw him over the parapet and kept him hanging there by his feet until the train had passed by only a short distance below. My grandfather was a bully and a thug who showed nothing but contempt for anyone who was weaker than himself.

Like many of his time my grandfather served in the First World War and he along with his brother Edward enlisted in the county regiment the Durham Light Infantry with my grandfather gaining the rank of sergeant. Both were posted to France and took their places in the trenches on the killing fields of Flanders. The carnage of the western front claimed the lives of millions of service men on both sides with every inch of ground repeatedly paid for with the life blood of those who understood little of the politics would condemn them to death. My grandfather's brother Edward Brown service No 366 of the 6th Battalion DLI, was one of those who made the ultimate sacrifice. He died on 10th September 1915 age 25 of wounds received at Flanders and was laid to rest at Bailleul cemetery.

Many of the fallen would be lost forever in the mud and shell holes that turned the French and Belgium countryside into a landscape of death and desolation. There would be no headstones to commemorate their sacrifice or testament to their passing, only a memory in the hearts and minds of their loved ones, and a blood red poppy on Remembrance Day. One such brave soul was little George ''Geordie'' Shaw who enlisted with my grandfather. A tiny man compared to my grandfather, and he like many service men looked to their sergeant for leadership and courage when theirs began to fail. On a cold damp morning before yet another pointless offensive that would claim countless lives, Generals far away raised a glass to a 'dashed good show', while little Geordie Shaw cowered between my grandfather's legs and begged him not to make him go over the top to his certain fate. When the officer's whistle blew it would sound the order to move forward towards the enemies lines. The sergeants would drive their men up the scaling ladders and forward into no man's land where death waited patiently for those foolish enough to trespass.

Onwards, towards the German lines through knee deep mud and water filled shell holes that stank to high heaven from the corpses of their already fallen comrades. My grandfather did his duty that day like all good soldiers did for a king and country so far away that appeared to have forgotten them. Geordie Shaw and many more like him died that morning without really understanding why.

Nat Brown returned from the war with his body intact but with a mind even more traumatised by the horrors he had witnessed. He carried with him the burden of guilt for men under his command that had died, whilst he had been spared to return to a life that could never be the same again. With his nerves shredded by what we know today as post-traumatic stress syndrome, he returned home and eventually went to see his doctor to ask for help. There would be no help forthcoming, what he received instead was the humiliation of being chased from the surgery by an irate doctor and told that a strapping man like him should be ashamed for saying he had trouble with his nerves. He had escaped the killing fields of Flanders but no good deed goes unpunished and now his own personal demon's had become entwined with the images of his darkest nightmares. With no medical help forthcoming he looked for succour and comfort in bosom of religion. The bosom and religion came into my grandfather's life in the form of a female captain in the Salvation Army with whom he had a long standing affair. The affair eventually became common knowledge but since he lacked finer feelings or moral standards, it's hardly surprising that fidelity didn't appear on his own personal radar. Later in life my mother would discuss the affair with me saying the captain adored my grandfather and described him 'as a strapping figure of a man'. Obviously her adoration was much stronger than her religious beliefs; she didn't allow her spiritual aspirations get in the way of her physical needs and Nat shaking her tambourine.

Age sometimes softens the edges of a person's personality but with Nat there were no such concessions; as he grew older the anger and hatred burned just as fiercely within him as it did when he was in his prime. Age afforded my grandmother no protection either as she continued to suffer terrible beatings into

40

her old age which only stopped when his health deteriorated to such an extent he was no longer able to raise his fists to her. No matter how old or infirm she was or how many times he beat her senseless Bella idolised him and always had a ready excuse for his brutal behaviour. A tiny woman who stood not much above five feet tall, who had known nothing but pain and hardship all of her life still loved and feared the man she married all those years before. In many ways such was my grandfather's personality and ability to instil fear and adoration in equal measure Bella was always in his shadow. No matter what hardships life threw at her she did what had to be done to get it done. When she lost three of her children in as many years she was able to find within herself the strength to carry on and eventually have more children. Bella was a simple woman who believed that once you made your bed you had to lie in it, even if the person you shared it with was a brutal monster. She was the home maker and the peace maker who put herself between her children and the man she loved when the madness came over him and he was out of control.

As a small child, I remember my grandfather sitting one day having a meal whilst I played on the floor, even in his old age he was still an imposing figure with a shock of white hair parted by a silver scar over his dark menacing eyes. Maybe I was making too much noise and disturbing his tea but for some reason he took off his thick black leather belt and shaking it in front of my face and growled 'this is what you get if you don't behave'. I must have looked scared because Bella stepped forward and told him 'stop it Nat you are frightening the bairn'.

My lasting memory of my grandfather would be from an old photograph. He and Bella took us to the seaside one summer and someone took a photograph of the two of them sitting in deck chairs on the beach with the kids playing in the sand. Nat sat there in his flat cap, dark woollen three piece suit, shirt and tie looking straight into the camera. The anger and hatred in his dark brooding eyes was as strong and intimidating as it had ever been. When the end came the cancer that began in his throat spread through his body and the pain became unbearable. My grandmother had to listen to him scream as wave after wave swept through his emaciated body. No one could have begrudged her a moment satisfaction as she watched him suffer. Yet all she found in her heart was compassion and the sorrow of losing the man she never stopped loving. She asked the doctor who was monitoring his condition if he could give my grandfather something to stop the pain and Nat Brown left this world in a state of peace that few if any would say he deserved.

I will come for you

When darkness prepares to release its hold for the final time I will come for you. The love I bring will replace your fear with peace and understanding.

As your time draws near I will lift the veil of tears so you may see once more your loved ones who have gone before. This is not the end; and amidst the anguish and sorrow of your leaving I will bring comfort to those who grieve your passing.

Whilst those about you are lost in their memories we will pass quietly amongst them as we prepare for your journey home. Those with eyes to see will witness your transition and the spirit of those who have come to escort you home. In that moment they will know the truth, and their pain and sorrow will be no more.

As if a thousand suns had risen by your command we will step into the light and you will be home once more. All hearts will be lifted and voices will be raised in celebration of your return, and what has gone before will be no more than a dream.

Chapter Four

❖❖❖

The fruit never falls far from the tree

❖❖❖

To understand my mother you have to understand the brutality she suffered and witnessed as a child. She grew up in a household where violence and aggression was a regular occurrence fuelled by her father's own mental illness and drink fuelled rages. From an early age she watched her mother being beaten sometimes to a bloody pulp. Witnessing her father's uncontrollable anger she quickly learned that violence and brutality were legitimate ways of handling everyday situations. If he'd had a bad day at work, if his meal wasn't to his liking or wasn't on the table when he wanted it, or any number of excuses to vent his anger and frustration someone would suffer the consequences. My grandfather wasn't a man to just slap someone if he was angry; neither was he a respecter of men women or children, he treat everyone with the same contempt and he spoke with his fists, no matter who he was venting his anger on.

He didn't soften with age. My brother once saw him when he was in his old age beating my grandmother who was a tiny woman not much more than five feet tall. My brother said he was frightening to watch as his face was contorted with uncontrollable rage, punching her with such ferocity it looked as if he wanted to kill her. The strange thing is no matter how much he hurt her, no matter how many times he beat her senseless she thought the world of him.

My grandfather was a big powerful man that hurt people because he could, and even those he considered friends called him 'a nasty piece of work' but made sure he never heard them say it.

If the constant threat of violence and the beatings weren't enough, my mother would have to contend with her mother's ignorance and fear. An incident as a child left her physically, emotionally and psychologically scarred for the rest of her life. My grandmother was working in her kitchen and had a pan of boiling water on the stove, whether the handle of the pan was sticking out is not known but the consequences of my mother reaching up and pulling the pan on top of her are all too clear and horrible to imagine. If that wasn't horrific enough what happened next was beyond belief. With the help of some neighbours my mother was held down on the kitchen table whilst the steaming wet clothes were ripped off the large blisters that had formed on her neck, shoulder and chest. With the neighbours pinning her down my grandmother set about bursting the blisters with a bar of carbolic soap. The trauma must have been unimaginable and she carried the horrendous scars for the rest of her life. If it's possible for one incident to trigger a mental illness then it's easy to see this being the one that tipped my mother over the edge into the dark abyss of depression and psychosis. At what age my mother's rage began to take control her life is unknown. The cause on the other hand is much easier to identify and if not the violence and abuse of her father then this horrific episode must surely have acted as a catalyst that fuelled the anger, frustration and uncontrollable rages throughout her life. This rage would spill out in such a way as to put her life at risk, and the lives of those around her.

This became a chilling reality when she was asked to baby sit one of her nephews who was still a child at the time. He was misbehaving and threw a bar of soap at my mother, hitting her in the face. There was no way anyone could know what was about to happen as he dived under the kitchen table to get out of her way. In that moment she lost all control. She reached under the table and pulled him out by his hair, as she did so she picked up a serrated bread knife and cut his throat. If it hadn't been for the intervention of her brother in law grabbing her hand as she cut the child's throat she would have surely spent the rest of her life in jail or a mental institution for murder. As it was he escaped with his life but carried a physical scar for a long time before it eventually faded. One day he recounted the story word for word and with more than a little pride showed me his neck where he came so close to dying having had his throat cut by my mother. The psychological scars may have lasted much longer than the physical ones, for later in life he himself would succumb to violent outbursts. As children my sister and I would be given the opportunity to witness my mother's anger first hand. My brother was about to have his throat cut and we were made to stand and watch. He was forced to sit on a chair where she grabbed him by the hair, pulled his head back and the put the knife to his throat. My mother was screaming uncontrollably, threatening to cut his throat if he ever misbehaved again. My brother was in tears and screaming in fear of his life. We were made to stand and watch as a means of being taught a harsh and painful lesson. What the lesson was I have no idea, but the memory and the screams I remember to this day.

My mother learned to fight at an early age. There were no handbags or hair pulling, she could hold her own with any man, stand toe to toe and trade punches blow for blow, which she did on many occasions. She was a product of a harsh environment and an even harder upbringing; she was by any standard as hard as nails. She had to be in order to survive. In my mother's mind if nowhere else the family name and her father carried a great deal of kudos and as such a reputation to uphold. She and her sisters were barred from some of the pubs and clubs in the town at one time or another. Whether this was because of them causing trouble or by reputation alone it's hard to say, but there was one specific incident that clearly showed their arrogance and total disregard for other people's safety or their property.

One of the many places they liked to drink was The Old Horse Shoe. Back then it had large ornate frosted glass windows that looked out onto the main road. One evening they were in there having a drink. Most if not all of pubs back then had open coal fires and this particular evening one of my auntie's decided the fire needed stoking up to warm the place up a bit. But instead of taking the time to find a poker to do the job properly like any normal person would do, she decided to pick up a bar stool and use one its legs to poke the coals to get the fire going. Obviously the landlord wasn't best pleased but when he tried to stop them he ended up sitting in the fire. The police were called but they took off before the police arrived. In my mother's damaged mind it was the landlord who was in the wrong. She stood over the road from the pub seething that he'd had the nerve to put them out of the pub and call the police. Instead of having the common sense to leave and get away she calmly walked back over the road and began to smash the pub windows with her bare fists. When she got to the windows that were toughened frosted glass, she simply removed one of her shoes and used it to help break the glass.

Although I can't remember how old I was I do remember that night for all the wrong reasons. I was being looked after by my grandmother and I remember my mother walking into the bungalow. She was wearing a light coloured rain coat with a tie belt and from the waist down the coat was literally soaked in blood. When she took her hands out of her pockets her hands and wrists were cut to ribbons. The strange thing is at that point my memory of that night stops abruptly. I don't know what happened from then on. Was she charged, did she get the medical treatment she needed I don't know. I appear to have blocked it out because it was just too traumatic to remember.

I claim my birthright.

I claim the right to learn all lessons in life with a smile instead of a frown, through the softly spoken word instead of the voice raised in anger. I claim my right to look at life through eyes washed with the sweet tears of laughter instead of bitter tears of remorse.

I claim my right to choose the path I walk and the lessons I am ready to learn. To walk gently through life avoiding the

50

pitfalls of adversity, tread softly upon life's experiences and listen to the words of wisdom in all things.

I claim my right to walk softly through life, accepting there is no more spirituality in hardship than in beauty. If there is a price to be paid for lessons, I claim my right to determine the value to be gained.

I claim my right to challenge adversity as the best teacher; experience is the greatest teacher of all. Through experience, we become our own best teacher, and in doing so we teach to others, what we wish to learn.

Chapter Five

Just one more for the road...

My mother liked to drink and get lost in that warm alcoholic haze that softened the edges of reality so she could no longer hear the voices or feel the pain. Unfortunately the alcohol helped to make her even more unpredictable, violent and aggressive. Years down the line when the prescribed amphetamines and barbiturates would take over her life she would swing from one extreme to another. From climbing the walls during withdrawal to near comatose drug induced stupor.

But in the early days it was the demon drink that drove her on and fuelled her violent outbursts. One of her favourite pubs in Crook was the Commercial Inn in Commercial Street. It was next to the railway crossings which extended out past the coal sidings we used to steal coal from. We walked up and down that road many a night in all weather whilst my mother drunk enough to forget and numb the pain. To forget the abuse she had suffered as a child and the burdening mental illness she carried for the rest of her troubled life. My brother would have been about eleven or twelve at the time and it was his job to push my sister who was still only a baby in her pushchair whilst I walked besides holding on the best that I could. Some nights if we were lucky my grandparents would look after us until closing time when my mother would literally stagger the short distance from the pub to their bungalow to collect us. We then had to walk across town to get home.

My mother grew up witnessing unspeakable acts of violence and suffered at the hands of both her parents. An accident as a child and the consequences of her mother's ignorance would leave her both physically and mentally scarred for the rest of her life. Her father's savage and uncontrollable temper was felt by men and women alike as he vented his anger on anyone who came close. It was a legacy passed down from my grandfather to my mother and it helped destroy her life. By today's standards as children we lived a life of constant abuse and deprivation but compared to my mother's childhood ours was idyllic.

As we grew up we would learn little by little some of the horrors she suffered at the hands of parents she hated, loved and admired in equal measure

Walk softly upon the earth

Child as you come into this world respect the old ways and walk softly upon the earth lest you disturb it with your passing. The mountains and high places will watch over your journey and the forests you love will wrap you in their coats of many colours as the season's record your passing. As you grow into a man honour and value all life for everything has its rightful place in the great scheme of things and is deserving of your respect.

Take time to give thanks to your own God and the spirits of those who have gone before you, for the blessings you will discover along the way. At all times look to nature and mother earth for guidance for we are all connected, she is the great teacher and how quickly you learn her lessons will determine how well you live your life.

Our tomorrows are neither certain or promised so in the fullness of life remember that our time here is short and we are merely visitors to these lands. Time, no matter how fleeting, can break the bond between you and the land who gave you life.

With the changing season's age will take it's time from you, in return will give you a life full to overflowing. Live it well; for in doing so your yesterdays will become precious memories worn and warmed by the passing of time to be enjoyed once again in moments of quiet reflection. For with the setting of your sun the circle of life will be complete.

Chapter Six

***

My journey began with small faltering steps

***

My own journey began in the early hours of May 11th 1951 when much to my mother's relief I was brought kicking and screaming into this world. While my birth may have come as a relief to my mother I was born into a relatively poor, broken and a very dysfunctional family in an old mining town of Crook on the edge of the Dales in County Durham, in the north east of England. This was a time of great austerity as the country was still struggling to recover from the effects of the Second World

War. A small rural town, Crook first appeared on the map as a tiny agricultural village around 1795. By 1835 agriculture had given way to a thriving mining industry; due to the vast coal seams which lay very close to the surface.

Sometimes so close it would break free to bruise and scar the surrounding landscape as the grass died back to reveal the precious coal beneath. At its height there were over 20 drift mines around the Crook area which led to a rapid growth in the population as people migrated into the area from far and wide to find work and hopefully improve their quality of life and standard of living. However the prosperity was relatively short lived as by the early 1900's the coal seams began to run out and the mines and dependant local industries started to close resulting in extreme hardship and poverty, with one in three of the remaining population being out of work. As time went on all that would be left of this once thriving industry was the rusting skeletal debris that dotted the landscape. These would eventually be removed for salvage or just abandoned and overgrown. It was if the land had waited patiently to remove all evidence of the mines, and reclaim what had been torn from it.

It was a hard and uncompromising life that claimed many lives. Some crushed and buried under tons of coal when the mine roof collapsed, but many more died later in life from black lung or miner's pneumoconiosis caused by breathing in the caustic coal dust. Coal was king and the mine owners become very wealthy, but the prosperity it provided for them came at a very high price to their workers. The hours were long, the work hard and dangerous with the 'ewers' having to dig out the coal with pick and shovel in claustrophobic eighteen inch high coal seams. They often worked in virtual darkness able to see no further than the glow emitted by the insipid light of their miner's lamps, hard thirsty backbreaking work with churches greatly outnumbered by the pubs and working men's clubs in the town. My family like many others weren't intentionally dysfunctional or poor; it was merely the result of social circumstances and their own values and experiences that made them the way they were.

Unfortunately, no one could know how that would impact on my life or the extent of the damage or the years of abuse we would suffer.

I don't have many memories of my earliest years other than a few scant mental images that may be genuine memories or the result of an over active imagination created by what was to become an increasing troubled, neglected and abusive childhood. Counselling and self development work later in life would confirm that many of my early memories were simply suppressed or blocked out as a coping mechanism. If you can visualise those memories as a reel of cellulose film with each frame representing an individual memory or childhood experience, some contain bright and clearly defined images, some show images merging with an encroaching darkness. Others are completely burnt out as if over exposed to some physical or emotional trauma that I couldn't deal with. I was advised during those early counselling sessions to avoid any kind of hypnotherapy as this may inadvertently cause the suppressed memories to resurface and I may or may not be able to deal with them. That's one part of my life I'm happy to leave well alone. What I do have is a little knowledge and understanding of what made my family the way they were. I say a little because some things I will never understand, as the people with the answers to many of my questions died long ago and took with them any hope of understanding the chain of events that began with my grandfather in 1886 and the effect it had on lives 132 years later.

Although my birth certificate shows I was born in Crook I spent a lot of time being dragged from pillar to post in all-weather between Crook and Cippenham near Slough in Buckinghamshire where my father lived. This was a place of farmlands and green pastures; of gentle streams and gentle ordinary people whose sedate lifestyle was totally alien to my mother who considered its people as weak and characterless. This constant tooing and frowing was due to my parent's volatile and stormy relationship which was caused to a large extent to my mother's violent nature and a mental illness. I would come to understand this illness as a personality disorder and manic depression, or bi-polar as its known today. My parents met when my mother was working as a general domestic in an isolation hospital not far from where my father lived. If he didn't already know the state of my mother's mental health, her true nature showed itself when a simple misunderstanding quickly escalated into a bloody and violent attack on an unsuspecting female work colleague. An innocent comment triggered her insecurities and she responded in the tried and tested fashion. In an instant uncontrollable rage took control of her and without warning grabbed the women by the throat and threw a barrage of punches leaving her face a bloody mess. She was restrained by a number of staff until she was able to calm down and gain some control over herself. It's not known if she left the hospital as a result of this incident, but she did leave and married my father.

When war broke out my father enlisted in one of the local regiments and was posted overseas. While he was doing his bit for king and country my mother was doing her bit for a long term boyfriend. On one of her many trips back home she became pregnant, and my half-brother was born just as the war was coming to an end. Her long term affairs and her fragile state of mind, the countless arguments and fights led to my parents getting divorced only to inexplicably remarry again, a classic example of can't live with you, but don't want to live without you.

My father being demobbed at the end of the war did little to help the situation. I was the result of an attempt to make the relationship work, but when my sister was born four years later it was uncertain who the father was and it was the beginning of the end. The many separations and endless fights eventually took their toll and their stormy and violent relationship finally came to an end in the late 50's when they agreed to go their separate ways for the last time. Although their marriage and relationship was finally over they never divorced. My mother's relationship with her boyfriend eventually came to an end, and she was left to raise the three of us on her own. My father met someone else but because he was still legally married his new partner changed her name by deed poll to Hawkins and they lived happily together as man and wife until my father suffered the heart attack that killed him a few days after his 45th birthday. My mother received a letter informing her of my father's death two months later. His will had been read and all of his estate went to his partner. My mother felt that she should have received whatever money and property my father owned as they were still technically married, but I think the letter she received was more than she deserved.

The Circle is Broken

Conceived in a moment of passion that cooled with the morning light, never to be rekindled a spark that burned so bright. Born into a world of danger protected in a warm embrace, held as a precious possession fear vanishes and leaves no trace

Those faltering steps of childhood from innocence to despair; love was used as a weapon by those who should have cared. The pain has gone; the damage done; now only the scars remain.

The strength of youth is fleeting it's gone before you realise; I grieved for my missing childhood seen through aging eyes. Within the man the child remains wherein the conflict lies and in the quiet of the night we remember with tear filled eyes.

As time rolled on I prayed for change, a dream for someone to care, a hand held out a silent plea I was alone, there's no one there. The walls I built for protection kept everything away, the reassurance I craved for, the words I needed you to say. When love I found I was unprepared and unable to respond, held captive by my own emotions afraid to venture beyond.

So many times you cried alone not knowing what to do, the hurt you felt the tears I caused and the anguish I put you through. Like the seasons I slowly changed and tried to make amends, the time had come to care, to give without remorse, the circle broken; my life could run its course.

In the night I'm no longer alone the joy of having you near, memories once painful are no longer held in fear. Life moves on the futures bright a family love and share, a hand held out for reassurance at last I know you are there...

Chapter Seven

Not every change offers a chance to rest

One of the first memories I can be certain of has been verified by others who shared the same experience so I know it actually happened. I also accept that all experiences and the memories they create are subjective, so even though we may share a childhood experience how we choose to remember it may be totally different. All I can do is share with you the recollections of a then five or six year old child whose life was about to be changed forever. As my parent's relationship fell apart I was spending more and more time with my father and the time with him was stable and to a large extent idyllic. It was a small village with its country style pub; a small stream meandered past the front door of our home down to the village duck pond.

After the war my father worked hard to make a new life for himself and his family. In spite of knowing my mother had been unfaithful and having my half-brother as a constant reminder he tried hard to make the relationship work. He tried his best to share his time between Crook and his home and provided my mother with a lovely house in Cippenham which she rejected only to return time and time again to the hardship and violence she was comfortable with. The war had changed everything, he realised he would have to learn new skills in order to make a living. He retrained himself and began working as a builder and plasterer eventually starting his own business. It was the way he threw himself into his work, and the stress caused by his marriage, I believe brought on the heart attack that killed him. My parents were spending more and more time apart and the relationship was deteriorating reaching the point of no return. This moment of realisation for my father came as a result of a very painful lesson learnt on one of his visits to Crook. The reason for the visit is uncertain; was it another attempt to make the marriage work or as I suspect something more serious, did he want to take me back to live with him. I will never know. What is known, he was severely beaten and it was made very clear to him it was just a taste of what would happen if he ever returned. Was my mother a part of this, did she know it was going to happen or worse instigate it. Again I will never know, but I can only imagine the physical and emotional pain he must have felt if those same thoughts went through his mind.

In the early days when I spent time with my father his family ensured my time there was stable and secure. They also ensured during the many separations all evidence of my mother presence including photographs were removed, which caused even more arguments and fights when she bothered to return. When my parents finally separated for the last time the stability I enjoyed with my father would be lost forever. I remember seeing my father for what would be the last time. We spent time together and when it was time for him to leave kissed me, said goodbye, and I never saw him again.

I returned to Cippenham in the late 1990's to re-establish contact with my father's family to try and understand why things turned out the way they did. An Uncle was the only one left who could effectively provide me with the answers and information I was looking for. We visited my father's grave, he recounted stories and took me to meet people who knew him, but when I asked about my mother's behaviour, he would only say 'it's wrong to speak ill of the dead' and the conversation was closed. The village where I spent the first few years of my life is still there albeit encase by modern day urban sprawl, the pub and the pond I recognised from an old photograph of my parents sitting outside having a drink with some friends. They were long gone, the pond was still there but its ducks were too young to remember me.

Difficulty is a door of opportunity

Life is uncertain; time and changes our constant companions. Time measures each step we take only to have our footprints erased by the winds of change that covers our passing as we move from one experience to another. Learning takes us into the unknown; a place of shadows and uncertainty where the light of knowledge and understanding are distant memories, and we feel lost and alone. Difficulty is the door of opportunity that stands before us, and in the distance voices call for us to trust and come to the edge of uncertainty.

Change is the guardian of the keep where in lies all that is, and all that we can be, if we would have the courage to find the key that unlocks the door. Comfort has grown cold about our shoulders as we inch ever closer.

Time stands beside us as we look for reassurance and hear nought but our own heartbeat synchronised with the echoing tick, tick, tick that measures our progress on life's journey.

Like the dawning of a new idea a candle glows before us, the flickering beacon of hope in the darkness, and within the flame the realisation that time and change are servants or our masters.

Difficulty is a door of opportunity that lies before us; we must find the strength and courage to enter into the darkness that shields it from us, and face the fear we carry within.

The smallest light illuminates the darkness of ignorance and fear and in doing so we are able to inch forward and eventually step once more into the light of knowledge and understanding.

Chapter Eight

Out of the fire and into the freezing cold

After that final separation when my mother returned to Crook we had nowhere to live. Up till that point our grandparents had helped raise us during our frequent trips north but theirs was a very unstable and violent relationship with my grandmother the victim of my grandfather's violent outbursts and beatings. It was this sustained violence and abuse that I think was a major contributing factor to my mother's mental health problems that developed at an early age, and her dependency on alcohol and prescribed medication later in life.

The breakup of her marriage and the breakdown of her relationship with her parents was the main reason our new home became an abandoned corrugated tin hut on the outskirts of town. These huts were collectively known as the Miners Hostels. This run down collection of huts and their residents were known locally as the 'squatters' and home to several families who were like us, homeless or waiting to be re-housed by the local council. These squats were Nissen huts that had been built to accommodate the ''Bevin Boys'' who worked in the few remaining local pits instead of serving in the forces during the Second World War. They were decommissioned in 1947 and stood empty until squatters moved in. This was discussed in the Houses of Parliament and a statement issued by the then Minister of Works was recorded in HANSARD on the 20th March 1951.

Nissen huts were constructed of arched corrugated sheets covered in tar that were sunk into the ground or secured to brick foundations at each side like a half buried tube. The ends were bricked up with a door at one end and a metal framed window at the other, several of these huts were linked by a central brick corridor that connected all of the huts in that particular block. Because they had stood empty for so long not everyone had access to electricity and some of the other basic amenities were either scarce or non-existent. One family who lived in a hut where the electricity supply had been disconnected spliced a makeshift cable from the main power supply to their hut, risking prosecution and electrocution, but harsh times called for harsh measures, and if you had a family to support and little or no money you did what had to be done to survive. One of my aunties had moved into the squat before us, so the hut we shared with her family was deemed to be 'their hut' and we were there under sufferance. To say it was basic would be stretching understatement to breaking point. The only source of heating was a small cast iron wood or coal burning stove at one end of the hut around which everyone would sit as close as they could just to keep warm. We would burn anything we could get hold of including furniture and tar off the roofs of other buildings.

If we didn't have what we needed we got it any way we could, including stealing coal from a nearby coal yard and railway sidings late at night so no one would see us. The hut was partitioned off so that both families lived in one end and slept in the other. Each family had their own bed in which adults and children regardless of age or numbers slept side by side and top to toe. When it was cold the beds would be piled high with overcoats or anything else we could find to keep warm and the cold at bay. We were lucky enough to have electricity for light but the stand pipe outside of the hut that provided water would freeze solid in winter. I can still remember standing there one bitterly cold winter's day with my mother in snow drifts that had blown into the passage through the broken doors and windows. We were burning newspapers trying to melt the solid block of ice that encased the tap and stand pipe. There was no chance of getting any water that day so we collected and melted snow to have something to drink and cook with.

The toilet during the day was where ever you could find a moment of privacy or a toilet that still worked properly. At night it was a communal bucket in the middle of the floor in the room where we slept. This would be slopped out the following morning, at the same time cleaning up spillages and misses of the night before.

Anyone who has spent time in a Nissen hut will know that you bake in the summer, freeze in the winter and when it rains you get wet from the inevitable leaks. There was many a time we woke up in the winter to see ice on the inside of the hut. On one occasion a visiting rat looking for somewhere warm to sleep tried to climb in bed with us. Luckily my aunt liked cats and there were several that seemed to come and go which was good because it helped deter the rats and mice from moving in on a permanent basis. When any of the cats died my cousins had a habit of burying them with the cat's tail sticking up out of the ground so they could remember where they had put them. When told to get rid of the tails they simply sliced them off with the spade and threw them away. Home comforts were few and far between, make do and mend was the order of the day and necessity being the mother of invention when we didn't have any cups, we simply drank out of jam jars or anything else we could find that was fit for purpose. At that point in time all of our possessions could be carried in a pram and no sooner had we settled in than we were loading up and on the move again. Violence played a major part in my childhood and formative years, not only was it considered acceptable it was expected and the chosen way of dealing with most if not all problems.

A hard life can create hard uncompromising people and members of my extended family appeared to revel in the reputation violence created and it wasn't long before my mother had one of her many stand up knock down fights, this time with my aunt and one of her sons. I was sat on the floor of the squat and for some unknown reason one of my cousins decided to stamp on one of my toys and break it, tempers flared and quickly escalated into a full blown knock down drag out fight between my mother, my aunt and her son. Whilst they were standing toe to toe trading punches I tried to help by jumping onto my cousins back and repeatedly punching him as hard as I could. Considering I was only about six at the time and he was a strapping teenager I don't think I worried him nor did much damage, in the process I was thrown across the room for my trouble. The pattern was always the same, something was said or done, tempers would flare, fists would fly and you are walking the streets again. I remember that particular night vividly; hanging on to the side of the pram walking towards the town centre with my mother and brother.

It appeared to be very busy and bathed with bright street lights, but we slept that night huddled in a derelict house that lacked doors or windows and very little roof. What it did have was a nosey neighbour who came out to see what we were doing. No help was asked for and none was given on that long cold night. The following day we were back at the squatters living in an uneasy peace. Childhood is supposed to be a happy time; growing up feeling safe and protected, learning from those around you who are supposed to love and care for you.

Unfortunately, they can only teach what they have learnt themselves and life was teaching me some very hard lessons. As well as suffering physical hardships I saw children I played with taken into care and people from the other huts arrested and taken away for whatever reason, but it was my mother who taught me some of the hardest lessons. I was playing with another child outside the squat when we started to argue over a broken metal toy. The argument led to a fight during which he raked the sharp edges down the side of my face leaving some nasty gashes, and faint scars visible to this day. Bloodied, in pain and frightened, I ran crying to my mother like any child would do looking for her to make it better. What I got was hit and screamed at for crying. Still bleeding, I was dragged outside and forced to beat the kid whilst she watched. I learned to fight my own battles, and he learned never to hurt me again. Only then did I get the attention I needed. The harshness shown to me as a child would be repeated time and time again, and each time my frustration, anger and hatred towards her would grow.

The Seeker's Prayer

Every challenge we experience gifts us the opportunity to go beyond what we already know about ourselves and take us into the unknown and discover what we are capable of. As we venture ever further into this strange land courage born of comfort and certainty recedes until it's no more than a cold distant memory.

In the emptiness our thoughts like unwanted echoes return again and again as the fear of failure gives life to the shadows of our mind.

Ever more uncertain we stumble over the remains of our past mistakes buried by the sands of time. Fearful of what lies ahead and seeking comfort we cling ever tighter to the remnants of our fragile successes as the winds of change look to tear them from our grasp.

Exhausted our energy spent; supplicant, we plead for a moment's peace, and in the eye of the storm the seekers prayer is answered. Amidst a stillness that comes from beyond silence, a realisation the shadows have passed and taken with them the debris of dead and decaying beliefs long outgrown.

What appeared in our darkest hour as a barren landscape has been transformed by the light of a new dawn into a canvas ready to receive that which we hold to be true. A challenge, a new skill waiting to be developed, a new strength to be tested or a new relationship waiting to be forged out of fear and uncertainty.

Change is uncomfortable, but development always lies in that distant land beyond the barriers and borders of limitation that we set ourselves. Sooner or later each one of us must make that journey to seek out the truth and to be all that we can be.

Chapter Nine

Stop moaning, you're not dead yet...

I don't know exactly how long we lived at the squatters but I can distinctly remember playing in the fields in the warm summer sunshine and freezing in the winter as the cold wind and snow found its way into every crack and broken window pane. I also remember walking the streets in all weather; there had been another fight and we were kicked out again. One winter's day we were walking the streets after it had been snowing heavily. With my little legs and my short trousers the snow probably appeared deeper than it was; the day was bright but bitterly cold. We were walking past a fish and chip shop when a relative came out of the shop carrying what seemed to me to be the biggest parcel of fish and chips ever. The aroma drifting out of the shop was so strong it could have picked me up and carried me away. Everyone in our family knew about her unstable state of mind, our homelessness but no help was asked for, and none was given. After taking a moment to say hello, she went home to her family with her fish and chips, as we continued to walk the streets until it got dark. I have never understood why family and friends who knew what was going on didn't appear to care enough to do something about it.

We were being neglected and abused, we should have been taken into care and my mother sectioned for her safety as well as our own, but no one appeared to do anything to help us. We never got the care we needed and she spent time in and out of a psychiatric hospital going from one nervous breakdown to another. The same hospital I would sign myself into in an attempt to deal with my own mental health issues. Maybe the help was offered but refused, I will never know. What I do know, as a child there is so much you can't possibly understand, unfortunately childhood ignorance and naivety helps to establish your beliefs and values and perceptions of life growing up. The quality of your childhood experiences can't help but influence and set the tone for the rest of your life.

We were eventually re-housed into prefabricated single tier house built to help with the housing shortage after the war.

They were only meant as a stop gap measure until more substantial housing could be built but some of them stood for years. I recently drove past where it used to be but it was demolished grassed years ago. The prefab was our first real home after the squatters. It was a modest house but looked and felt like a palace by comparison, but this created all sorts of new problems. We weren't used to nice things and we didn't seem able to adjust and handle the changes. A nice home appeared to make her even more unstable.

It was like constantly living on a knife edge; it was much later in life I would come to realise the underlying problem wasn't the new house; it was my mother's mental illness and her inability to cope with the normal problems and pressures of life. Her personality disorder and Bi-Polar meant she was unable to deal with the everyday life. We moved from house to house often with no money, little or no food, even less furniture and bare floor boards. Her illness and addictive personality affected our childhood and in many ways continues to do so, albeit now in a much more positive life enhancing way. When I think back I did have some happy childhood memories but this was only when I was away from my mother and the toxic environment she created. Away from home I could escape and in the process achieve a certain amount of normality, but when the time came to go home the closer I got the darker and more depressed I became.

Walk softly upon the Earth

Walk softly upon the earth lest you leave evidence of your passing. Our time here is short and we are merely visitors in our own land. Our tomorrows are neither certain or promised; our yesterdays nothing more than shadows given life by the light of the morning sun. The mountains and high places watch over our journey; the forests wrapped in their coat of many colours as the season's record our passing.

As you go respect all life for each has its time and place in the great scheme of things; give thanks to your own God for the blessings you may find along the way.

At all times look to the children for they are your teachers, how well you learn their lessons will determine how well you live your lives.

In truth all are connected; the teacher and the student are one. In your haste take time to remember that this journey is just one that you have chosen to experience in order to develop and grow; you are the prodigal child who will one day return to your spiritual home.

Chapter Ten

We were the people I wouldn't have wanted for neighbours

Because of her violent and irrational behaviour mixed with some general anti-social behaviour on our part we were the family you shouldn't have to put up with as neighbours. My brother who had more than his fair share of issues to deal with owned an air rifle and would think nothing of taking pot shots at the neighbours out of the bedroom window. More than one was shot at as they worked in their gardens or walk past the house. A neighbour three doors away was a keen gardener and the sight of him bending over in his garden was just too much of a temptation for my brother to resist. At that distance the target was just too good to pass up, and a little too large to miss.

The strange thing was, the more settled we were the more irrational and unstable my mother became. It was a contradiction that I didn't understand and it would be many years later when I would finally begin to understand that the normality and stability were alien to her and she simply had no idea how to deal with it in a positive way. She didn't know how people behaved or reacted to everyday challenges in ways that didn't involve anger and violence. As she got older drugs overtook her life and she lost the physical ability to fight in the way she used to. Her anger and resentment turned in over and she became bitter and twisted. Where once she would let her fists do the talking she now used her tongue to inflict as much damage as she could and we all suffered as she vented the pent up anger and hatred. With her physical and mental health on a steady decline our home life began to deteriorate even further.

Later in life I returned to visit my brother after being away from that part of my life for many years. I was amazed how narrow the streets appeared and how small the houses actually were. Built in the forties the houses provided the luxuries of electric lights and indoor plumbing whilst retaining the old world charm of coal fires in the living room and bedrooms to provide heat and hot water. They also came with an outside toilet that froze up in the winter. A coal house and outside toilet in the yard at the back of the house, eventually we would be introduced to the luxury of toilet paper but my lasting memory of that outside toilet was a dark cold damp place with squares of newspaper fastened on a nail in the wall to use instead of toilet paper.

For goodness sake child, go outside and play

'For goodness sake child, go outside and play' magic words to my small ears and I didn't need to be told twice. 'Don't run and don't slam the door', my Gran would shout as I set off as fast as my little legs could carry me.

Of course I ran and the door did slam as it always did, followed by Gran's knowing smile and the shake of her head as I disappeared out the door and into a child's world of magic and make believe. Those magic words heard now a life time later, still have the power to take me back in time and I'm a child again escaping from the world of grownups to explore a world free from limitations and full of wonderment. When I had no one to play with nature became my friend and companion. The wind was the gentle voice of the trees whispering through the tinkling murmur of the leaves that acknowledged my return to the lands of make believe and far away.

The meadow grass danced and swayed to the rhythm of the warm summer breeze. The sun beams ebbed and flowed across a beautiful sea of green grass, its gentle sigh falling away like receding waves washing pebbles on a distant shore. Streams of mirrored glass held within them natures many colours. Slow and gentle in the morning light, they still had the power to carry with them a child's dreams and drop sticks to lands far away. Gentle pools no matter how small became portals to worlds of pirates or knights in shining armour. The mundane became the miraculous, with multi coloured pebbles giving hours of pleasure, a treasure worth a king's ransom. Sunbeams and not rainbows marked the pot of gold and all manner of hidden treasures waiting to be discovered.

The sunshine covered the land in its warmth; its glow cascading down through the trees whose branches like giant fingers reached out to catch and hold onto natures beautiful warm embrace. While canopies basked in brilliant sunshine even the smallest leaf was under lit with a golden glow that silhouetted the dust motes and insects whose dance rose and fell with the breeze on those hazy summer days. Sunbeams captured through squinting eyes saved for another day in jars and rusty tins, hidden in secret places long forgotten patiently awaiting their rediscovery. Back then I was able to see the wonder in all things through eyes that hadn't been clouded and dulled by age; time stood still as I held court with real and imaginary friends and ruled a world that for some reason only we alone could see.

We were safe in its embrace; protected by our own innocence and by a veil of forgetfulness that covered the eyes of those who no longer believed in the lands of make believe and far away.

Camps that were our castles and kingdoms were no more than twigs and drift wood to those who were unable to see the wonder before them. When we saw treasure and precious stones at our feet, the dust of life's experience kept them safe from those who had forgotten what it was like to be a child. The puddles we sailed to far distant shores led them to imagine nothing more than dirty footprints on a kitchen floor. When nature changed her coat of many colours she covered the land with autumnal hues that glowed like burnished copper in the morning sunshine. Her cool damp air gave rise to the mists of the dragon's breath, but soon the leaves that were once so vibrant and green would begin to fall and carpet the land to wither and die. My time for playing outside was quickly coming to an end.

The trees no longer whispered to me, their voices had grown silent; looking empty and lifeless as if robbed of their spirit as one by one their leaves broke away from their branches and fell to their death. As if in mourning the sunlight leached away into the ensuing darkness that became night long before it should. With the drawing in of autumnal nights came more and more time spent indoors. Fires banked up with coal and logs hissed and crackled as their sparks tried to escape the flames that were eager to consume them, warm clothes and even warmer soup in ready supply. Coats piled high on beds to keep us warm when the roaring fire was spent and its dying embers did little to keep the cold from creeping in under the cover of darkness. The days of playing in the sunshine were now no more than a distant memory to a child peering out through frost covered windowpanes into a cold and unforgiving night.

Crisp morning mists frosted the landscape as autumn surrendered its hold to the icy grip of winter; fluffy white snowflakes slide past metal grey skies and settle silently onto the land. Flake upon flake until the land relents and gives up its shape to accept a deep blanket of snow that glistens like a million stars. Trees sag under the weight as if dressed in ermine and hung with crystals in preparation of the coming celebrations; the only sound to break the silence is the breeze that moves effortlessly between the snowflakes to lead them on a swirling dance.

In the grey morning light nothing stirs; even the wind is late to rise on this cold but beautiful winter's morning. I sit with my nose pressed up against the window pane and feel the cold air on my face as it tries to find a way into the warmth. I try to follow flakes as they float past only inches from my face; as if to help some seem hover before moving on only to be replaced by others in such a hurry to become part of this white mantle that covers everything in sight. The land has long given up its shape, harsh lines are now softened and blend into the landscape and it's hard to see where the land ends and the sky begins. Only a *few broken fence posts like blackened fingers reach out of the snow as if to break free from winter's icy grip.*

My time outside was short but well spent and now a snowman stood guard. His coal black button eyes, nose and mouth were in sharp contrast to his pale waxen face that was framed with an old hat and scarf to keep him warm. Silent and impassive looking into the distance watching for the signs when winter would begin to leave and return to her lands far away. As if angered by his presence the icy winds scoured him with sleet and snow, his hat vanished in the night and his scarf frozen stiff like a broken and disused sign still trying its best to point the way. Eventually cold nights began to give way to pale watery mornings. Days without snow became more frequent and the land reclaimed some shape and definition as the snow began to recede and seep away across the still frozen earth.

Slowly the morning sun regained its strength and its colour returned. Our breath no longer misted in the cold air and his job done the snowman left us, his scarf and the coal the only reminder of the time he spent with us. Spring crept up cautiously as if unsure of what it would find. Small pools of snow and ice shaded from view still littered the landscape like forlorn stragglers forgotten and left behind as winter fled. Wellington boots stood in pools of water under coat hooks full to overflowing with coats, hats and scarves. In returning spring had uncovered the remains of autumns fallen, the debris and leaves that laid hidden so long now clung to our feet and trailed dirt across a clean kitchen floor. Slowly the air warmed, the land dried and brought with it a fresh new beginning that could be heard in bird song and seen in the pale green hues that heralded new life and new growth.

No matter how hard I tried those days were always awake before me; but like good friends they waited patiently for me to rise and get ready for school and the chores that ate into our time together. The silence of winter had given way to a dawn chorus and the sounds of the summer, nature now resplendent in all her glory covered the land with her coat of vibrant colours and even the house seemed happy to be alive.

As if summer were an honoured guest preparations were made to welcome it into our home. Doors and windows were thrown open and the sunlight mingled with the sounds of laughter and the heady aroma of freshly baked bread. Time was too precious to just walk and as if afraid to lose a moment it was chased after like a friend in play, doors slammed shut as if to keep it captive and saved for another day. Above the noise my Gran's voice loud and clear but warm and soft as those summer days, 'For goodness sake child, go outside and play'

Chapter Eleven

It's a fine line between love and hating you...

I loved my mother because she was my mother but I was afraid of her and I hated who and what she was. I also hated myself for the way I felt inside. Nothing in our lives seemed to be normal, we appeared to be different to other people and I hated the way that made me feel because I didn't want to feel different. I wanted to be a normal teenager living a normal life with normal parents but nothing could have been further from the truth. Due to her many problems my mother could at times, look and act very strange, appear frightening and intimidating. The alcohol and medication affected her speech, her balance and her behaviour, which usually resulted in disapproving stares or comments from those around her. The result was always the same; anger abuse or violence towards anyone who dared look at her or pass comment.

I was ashamed and I grew more ashamed of the way she looked and behaved the shabby dirty house we lived in with its bare walls and floors, and its untidy overgrown garden. We had moved on in so many ways, but the experience of living in the squatters seemed to cling to us like a bad smell and affect the way we lived. We were living in a three bedroom house, but to begin with we all slept in one bedroom and peed in a bucket under the bed. At times we used the bath as a toilet even though there was an outside toilet just a few feet away from the back door. Growing up with this feeling of isolation helped create a great deal of anger and frustration that I couldn't understand or express in a positive way, as a result my health suffered and I began to experience the onset of depression at a very early age. This sense of isolation was made worse by my family who I felt openly treat my brother differently to me.

As I grew up I became more and more convinced in my own mind that we were different in some way. As I grew older I felt an outsider in my own family and I began to rebel and lash out which only intensified my feelings of isolation. A shadow of that feeling clings to me even now as I see people I have little in common with and no real emotional connection to.

Love Is

Love is so precious it can't be bought; money can't buy what must be freely given. Love is a gift asking us to accept the present with gratitude and thanks. Love is a moment that has no memory of the past, it thinks of only what is and what can be. Love is timeless and limitless; once felt it holds us forever, yet forgives and releases in a moment.

Love is forgetful of mistakes yet remembers everything that makes love possible. Love is strong and powerful; it protects and keeps us safe, but responds to tenderness and the gentlest touch.

Love is patient and understanding of our ability to return its gift, and happy in all that it receives. Love is free of conditions; a precious gift wrapped up in our hopes and dreams. Given with thanks and received with gratitude.

Chapter Twelve

A new dawn, a new day, a new life, but the same old problems

If the squatters represented physical hardship then our time in Beech Avenue was a time of increasing mental torture for my mother when the drink was supplemented by a wide range of prescribed medication. It was then that the lives of my brother, sister and I began to disintegrate to such an extent that we all became selfish, isolated and introverted in order to cope with the madness that we found ourselves living in. My brother witnessed more of my mother's decline into mental illness than I did. To cope he lost himself in hard work gaining what pleasure he could from the things he wanted to do with little or no thought for the needs and feelings of others. Time softened those hard edges and with all of his faults he was well liked and I never met anyone who had a bad word to say about him. When he died years later the church was full to over flowing with people who wanted to pay their respects to a man who was loved and well liked.

I looked for my answers in drink. I became angry and isolated lashing out and hurting people because I could, and getting hurt more often than not in the process. I had attitude but lacked the ability to kick ass in any meaningful way. I began to follow the well trodden path of prescribed medication to deaden the pain, and in hind sight I was without realising it, trying my best to self-destruct.

We of the Forest path

We of the forest path are guides who show the way; we are the oracles of the woods that speak the language of nature, and hear the voice of mother earth. We have been present since time begun, and have watched nature in all its glory bring forth life through the cycle of her seasons. We were at the dawning of the standing stones; we stood upon high, and sang the praises of those who honoured the spirit of creation.

96

Life comes in many forms; each has its part to play, separate yet indivisible a spiritual tapestry that binds us together. The beauty of life that surrounds us; nature in all of its glory is ready and willing to help us recognise our own spiritual birthright. Spoken softly on a summer breeze or through the power of a raging storm, the wisdom of creation speaks to us if only we have the desire to listen.

The light of creation shines within us all; it is the signature of the life force that brought all things into being, we are because it is. We share our time and space with the rest of creation; but no matter how bright we shine we are only one of the many stars in the heavens. Our time is now; but ours is the briefest of moments compared to the mountains, the seas and the earth that gifts us life.

Spiritual maturity is a precious gift that must be earned to be appreciated; we must have the eyes to see, and the ears to listen to the kindred spirits that share our world. There are many dimensions to knowledge and understanding; the splendour of the mountains, the mysteries of the oceans, and the wisdom of the forest patiently awaits your arrival.

We must make our own journey; the forest path allows us to walk in peace and solitude, and rest for a moment at the feet of great teachers. Those with the heart to hear and understand are kindred spirits who walk the forest path.

Chapter Thirteen

Those pills didn't work, let's try the pretty blue ones

As my mother got older her health went into steep decline. The drink stopped doing what it needed to and it was around this time that she began to rely heavily on prescribed medication to supplement her drinking and help to get through each day. At one point her mental state was so fragile she admitted herself into a psychiatric hospital for treatment but then discharged herself, but her brief spell in hospital didn't stop the decline or uncontrollable violent outbursts. Initially she was prescribed various low strength antidepressants such as Valium and Librium as a means of controlling her behaviour. As her body became more and more used to the medication the strength and dosage had to be increased to help control her condition. When that failed to achieve the desired effect different types of amphetamines and barbiturates were tried, sometimes with disastrous effect. One of the medications the doctors experimented with was an amphetamine which my mother affectionately called her 'purple hearts'. It was far from affectionate and had disastrous results. The tablets were neither purple nor heart shaped but these tiny blue triangles had a frightening and powerful effect on her. She was manic, acting like she had been hard wired into the mains, at the same time dying on her feet from physical and mental exhaustion.

As time wore on she had to take more and more medication to try and maintain the same level of sedation. What started out as one capsule at night ended up with her taking six or more a day? A months' supply was often taken in less than a week and when she had none of her own medication left I would be sent out to buy more for her from people she knew where taking similar types of medication. I was ten years old at the time. I would be sent to certain addresses on the estate with a note and money in my hand to buy barbiturates or anything that was available to keep her going. I would knock at the door and hand over two envelopes. One contained a note and the other money; a short time later I would be given an envelope back which contained tablets of some description that would hopefully help her through her withdrawal symptoms.

100

One of the side effects of her personality disorder was that she was extremely paranoid. This was the main reason she made us all sleep together in one room. It was also why she always slept with a hammer and a carving knife in easy reach and a pepper pot under her pillow. These precautions were in case someone tried break into the house and kill us. Although highly unlikely, in my mother's damaged mind this was a real and present danger. She could go from nought to a hundred on the rage scale in a split second with little or no provocation. Late one night in the middle of one of these violent episodes made worse by drink and medication, she took both the hammer and knife out into the street screaming at the top of her voice daring any of the neighbours to come out of their houses and stop her.

This was just one terrifying example of my mother repeating what she as a child had seen her father doing. Instead of a hammer and knife, my grandfather would drag my grandmother along the street by her waist length hair, punching her, beating her face to a pulp, daring anyone to come out and stop him. Because of his size, his violent nature and reputation no one dared. Human nature being what it is I feel sure once that particular pattern of violence had been established many of the neighbours would have simply hidden in their homes so they didn't have to watch or listen to my grandmother screaming as she was beaten senseless.

Prayer of Guidance

Let the spirit of creation bless you with the wisdom that comes from knowledge and understanding. At every opportunity give thanks for the blessings you have received through its love and kindness. Let your actions cherish and respect the earth, the wonders of nature, and the magic of its creation. Walk softly lest you mark the earth with your passing and look kindly upon the beauty that lies before you.

Find the courage to be all that you can be whilst respecting the needs and desires of others. At all times try to live in peace with mankind no matter what their colour or creed, and honour their beliefs as you do your own. Tomorrow is neither promised nor certain; waste not your time regretting the past or fearing the future. Live your life to the full, do only what you can then let go and rest in the knowledge that you have done your best.

Chapter Fourteen

Bad luck is better than no luck

In what seemed a short space of time, death visited my family on three occasions. He called for me but I was out at the time and escaped more by luck than good management. In 1959 my grandfather died of cancer. He was in such agony that my grandmother begged the doctor to give him something to stop the pain. The doctor explained he could but if he did my grandfather would fall into a deep sleep and not wake up again. She said she understood and my grandfather slipped away in a state of peace that some may say he didn't deserve because of the pain and suffering he had caused so many people in his lifetime.

After my grandfather's death my grandmother eventually moved in with us, this created even more pressure and anxiety because her health was failing and my mother was in no fit state to look after herself never mind anyone else. In 1960 my father died of a massive heart attack a week after his 45th birthday. Around the same time my appendix decided that it would be a good time to kill me.

I was in a lot of pain for quite some time and our GP had repeatedly dismissed it as growing pains. My grandmother who believed in old fashioned remedies prescribed liberal doses of castor oil to sort the problem out, thankfully my mother didn't listen but my condition got gradually worse. On the fateful day the pain was so intense I could hardly stand and walking was virtually impossible. My mother being made of sterner stuff decided that I had to walk the length of our street to the doctor's surgery; we set off with me doubled over and sobbing with the pain. Half way up the street a miracle happened; the pain abruptly stopped, I was able to straighten up and continue to journey to the doctors without any discomfort. What neither my mother nor I realised was that the reason the pain had stopped was my appendix had burst and peritonitis was beginning to set in as the toxins started to spread through my young body.

The doctor's surgery was at the top of our street and after the short time it took to walk the length of the street we arrived at the surgery and took our place in the waiting room where we sat waiting to see the doctor. In those days there wasn't an appointment system or a receptionist and you saw the doctor on a first come first served basis. After several other patients had gone in to see the doctor it was our turn and we went into the treatment room sat down opposite his desk and explained what had taken place. The Doctor was a small dapper man who dressed very formally in a smart three piece suit and smoked a cigarette in a long cigarette holder. Looking over the top of his glasses he listened intently as my mother explained what had happened as we walked to his surgery. He paled slightly, politely excused himself and left the room. Unbeknown to us made an emergency phone call for an ambulance. What I didn't know at the time was how serious my condition was and how much danger I was in. Within 10 minutes I was in an ambulance on my way to Bishop Auckland hospital eight miles away with their two's and blue's ringing and flashing for all they were worth. On arrival I was prepped and taken straight to theatre where they operated on me and saved my life.

Although the operation was a success the procedures of the 50's and 60's weren't as technically advanced as they are today and it would take a further operation in 2000 to 'tidy up' the internal scar tissue left behind when my appendix burst.

I was eight or nine years of age at the time and while I was recovering from the operation a nurse came into the room and asked how I was feeling and would I like anything to read to help pass the time away. Apparently I said 'some days are better than others, some days I'm up and some days I'm down'. I then asked for a bible to read. My response caused sufficient concern that she reported my comments to the other nursing staff and my mother when she came to collect me. I also remember having to get the stitches cut out which left me with a very painful memory and a large ugly scar as a record of my lucky escape.

A short time later my grandmother's health began deteriorated and she died on a bed in our living room. Life carried on around her as we watched her shrink before our eyes, first her colour left her, and then her life drained away? I seem to remember her laid there, her mouth open and her tongue curling up and turning black.

Those who would hold us to mediocrity

Those who would hold us to mediocrity and convince us of our inability to achieve greatness make liars of us all. Those who would believe them make liars of themselves.

Chapter Fifteen

A school of hard knocks and shitting myself

School and I just didn't mix. School to me wasn't an enjoyable experience and the memories are less than happy, with good ones few and far between. In hindsight it was always a feeling of not fitting in and not being good enough. Being different, always on the outside looking in, spending time and energy trying to be something I wasn't just so I could fit in. Hindsight like experience is a wonderful thing that's never available when you need it the most, and looking back school for me was for the most part a frightening and stressful experience. School can be a tearful experience for both the child and the parent. For the parent their child is growing up and beginning their journey in life, for the child it can be overwhelming, handed over to strangers in a new and bewildering environment. This was 1956 and there weren't any playgroups, nurseries or preschool groups to ease the transition from home to education. One day you were at home getting under your mothers feet, the next you were surrounded by strangers in a strange environment where routine and discipline were the norm.

This in itself was a recipe for disaster as my short young life was never normal and routine and discipline was totally alien to me. There may have been tears in my mother's eyes but I was too busy fighting to notice. How the fights started I don't know, but I ended up fighting more than one child all at the same time. Most parents would have been horrified, but my mother was overcome with pride at her little boy sticking up for himself. Unfortunately this appears to have set the tone for my time in the infants and for the rest of my time in main stream education. In later years I would progress from fighting pupils to fighting teachers, and carrying a knife in school. That is until an older pupil, with a larger knife showed me the error of my ways.

I was an unruly child who just didn't fit in; constantly rebelling against the discipline of the school environment. If my first day fight was the highlight of my introduction to education, the low point had to be when my brother was called to take me home because I had soiled myself.

I can still remember walking out of the school gates holding my brothers hand, me in my little shorts, with shit all the way down my legs. I know was crying because I was cold wet and uncomfortable not to mention smelling to high heaven, but I was also scared of getting punished off my mother for dirtying myself. The strange thing is, like many of my stressful childhood memories I can remember so much and then there is nothing, it's like the experience was simply switched off and no longer existed. Children can be very cruel and so I can only image the teasing, torment and name calling that followed that day. I can't begin to imagine how ashamed my brother must have felt having to come and collect me then walk the distance through the streets to get me home to the squatters where we were living at the time. Experience gained later in life working with people who had been abused helped me realise all the signs were there at an early age and something was seriously wrong in my young life. Signs that should have been picked up on and addressed but unfortunately social services in the mid 1950's weren't as prevalent as they are today so a lot of abuse and neglect was simply accepted as ''normal'' or went unreported and undetected.

It's fair to say I never achieved anything at school and I went from junior school to secondary school in the 'C' grade which was known as the dunce's class. Along with the stigma of being less than bright I also qualified for free meals which identified you as poor as well as stupid. I left school at the age of 16 with a basic education level far lower than it should have been with a particular teacher's words ringing in my ears that I was thick and stupid and would be lucky to get any job. For many years I lived that truth until the age of 35 when things began to change. I attended college to gain a supervisory management qualification and prove to myself and others that I was far from thick or stupid. Thirty one years on and I'm still studying and gaining both experience and qualifications every chance I get.

There were many good teachers back then but there were also abusive teachers who obviously hated their jobs and hated the children in their care. With some teacher's their use of physical abuse was common practice. Striking pupils on the back of the head as they walked past their desk then grabbing hold of them by their hair and dragging them out of their seat was a daily occurrence. Some teachers were partial to throwing wooden board erasers across the room, and hitting the pupils with everything from books, shoes, cricket bats to straps and canes. All of which would prevent you from working in a teaching profession today, back then it just seemed to be accepted as the norm and very few if anyone had the courage to object or complain. Many years later I would bump into a couple of teachers that had taken a great pleasure in dishing out the many forms of corporal punishment and I was amazed at how they appeared to have shrunken both physically and psychologically. They were no longer the ogres that instilled such fear. Even the school buildings themselves appeared smaller and far less intimidating and bore little resemblance to the vast buildings I remembered.

One thing I have learned working with people who have survived an abusive childhood is many develop an acute sense of injustice which appears to come from the feeling of being powerless. I spent most of my childhood living in an atmosphere of fear and anger; as a result I developed a real hatred of any kind of injustice real or imaginary. Being treated unfairly I would fight against it, regardless of what the outcome would be. Back in the day if you were eligible you got free meals and school milk. The milk came in small bottles that were delivered to the school by the local milk man who stacked the milk crates in the school yard close to the school kitchens. No matter how hectic the school yard was you could always hear the rattle of the milk crates and the chinking of the bottles above the noise. This day I was hanging around that area of the yard with some others and as we were stood next to the milk crates and for some reason I picked a bottle of milk out of the top crate before putting it back down, the bell went and play time was over and we all trooped back into school for our next lesson and I never thought anymore about it.

Someone had taken some milk out of the crates and it was reported to the headmaster that I was the one that had been seen taking milk. I was pulled out of class by the headmaster and told in no uncertain terms that I had stolen the milk and was going to be punished for it. I was innocent and my initial fear was quickly replaced by anger. The headmaster's tirade quickly turned into a confrontation as I made it quite clear I hadn't done anything more than pick the bottle up before putting it back into the crate, I hadn't stolen anything and I wasn't going to be punished by him or anyone else. Obvious frustration got the better of the headmaster and he tried to get hold of me, I reacted in kind and sent him flying before taking off and getting out of school as quickly as I could. All of this had been witnessed by other pupils and so the word quickly spread that I had hit the headmaster before taking off. This may have looked good, but it did nothing to help the situation.

My mother was contacted and eventually I was marched back into school for a meeting with the headmaster during which he informed us that I must be punished because he would lose face if I wasn't. After further arguments it was agreed that I would do several hundred lines the content of which have been long forgotten.

I don't think I was anymore rebellious than anyone else. I did however carry a knife at school for a short while. Not because I thought it was cool, clever or threatening, I just couldn't see anything wrong with walking around with a sheath knife fastened to my belt. When one of my teachers found out they simply said they didn't think it was a good idea and someone could get hurt. That person was me. An older pupil who carried a much larger knife decided to show me how easily the point of his knife could go through my jacket sleeve and into my arm. To call it a wound would be verging on the ridiculous but the incident created sufficient concern to ensure there were no more knives carried in school.

Aiki Prayer

As I struggle to learn and grow judge me not on who I am, but consider who and what I can become. Don't let me take pride in success or fear failure for they are both meaningless comparisons. Above all else, bless me with understanding for with it I am at peace with myself. In understanding there is peace and harmony and the knowledge that the power of the universe guides my faltering steps. We are all on a journey of discovery; give me the strength and courage to help my fellow travelers on their road to fulfillment.

Chapter Sixteen

―◆◆◆―

The beginning of the end

―◆◆◆―

Sometime during the late 60's my life started to unravel. I was spending more and more time drinking to blot out the pain and suppress the simmering anger and frustration that had been building up for years. I was popping prescribed medication most days to keep the depression under control and drifting into petty crime to provide the money to buy the drink I needed to numb my brain that would stop me thinking and feeling. I remember walking the streets late one night and passing a woman making her way home on her own. As I passed her by I mumbled a slurred goodnight but for a few brief moments I saw her not as a person but as a means to an end and a way of making some easy money. I stopped and turned to watch her walking away thinking how easy it would be to snatch her bag and be gone before anyone was the wiser. Something stopped me and those thoughts left me as quickly as they came. I stood in the shadows and watched her walk away and disappear into the darkness.

My relationships at the time were intense and uncomfortable for everyone concerned because no matter where I was or who I was with I always felt alone and on the outside looking in. I was unable to make any real connection to people, even those I wanted to care about. Such was the intensity of the anger hatred and poisoned emotions such sensitivity and perceived weaknesses were burned away at a very early age. Today the scars remain and the damage so complete there is still part of me that love hasn't yet reached. I was incapable of holding a job down for any length of time largely due to the fact that any kind of meaningful structure discipline and routine were totally alien to me. My mother's advice was if you don't like the job or don't want to work you don't have to. Even when I found a job I enjoyed it usually didn't last long. When I was asleep she would turn my alarm clock off so that I would sleep in, continually be late for work get fired, and be at home to look after her. She looked after her mother when she was old and infirm and she honestly believed that our purpose in life was to look after her. As we grew up she did everything in her power to destroy any relationship that threatened her control over us.

She spent years trying to destroy my brother's marriage with her lies and deceit, when that failed she resorted to the tried and tested violence and intimidation. Although she tried her best she was never able to come between my brother and his wife and split them up, but she did leave a legacy of bitterness and hatred that even after her death took years for the damage to be repaired. In truth the scars never fully healed and it didn't take much to open old wounds.

My sister was the youngest and she never stood a chance. Her life was effectively destroyed by my mother. Her influence was so strong her first marriage was doomed before it even had a chance to succeed. Such was her power and control my sister accepted her as her role model and surpassed all of my mother's expectations. Sadly she would succeed to such an extent that my mother gained a protégé but we lost a sister at a very early age and our relationship was broken beyond repair. I would eventually foster, and then adopt two of her children as my own to stop them having the kind of childhood we had suffered. Instead of healing wounds it served only to provide my sister with what she perceived as a legitimate target to blame for all of her troubles. Sometimes love isn't enough and you have to just walk away and accept that some things once broken can never be repaired or put back together again.

As the drink and the drugs started to affect my mother's health she became a virtual recluse only leaving the house when she had no choice, this was partly due to the fact she had gone from being an attractive young woman in her youth to someone who in later life attracted stares and attention for all of the wrong reasons. Her general health problems left her with a drawn and haggard expression, this coupled with a diet of drink and drugs and a suppressed appetite left her looking strange wild eyed and at times quite frightening. From an early age I had to help my brother take on the role of carer, I was running errands to buy her drugs to stop her climbing the walls as she came out of her stupor and withdrawal symptoms that kicked in after taking a month's supply of barbiturates in less than a week.

When we had no money which was more often than not, I would be sent to get shopping without the money to pay for it and told to ask for it on account. I still remember the embarrassment and shame I felt as it was refused time and time again and the shopping taken off me in front of a shop full of customers. She either couldn't understand how embarrassed or ashamed I may have felt or she simply didn't care. Each time my hatred grew. Those experiences would be repeated time and time again as I was growing up and each time a little more anger and frustration would build up inside of me. There was no way of knowing the time would come when after years of abuse I would finally snap and try to kill her for everything she had put us through. Having thought better of it just in the nick of time and thus keeping her alive and myself out of jail I would later let the drink and medication do their worst as I tried to commit suicide.

This was more a plea for help than a sense of guilt, or an attempt to escape from reality.

Growing up with the kind of role models I had around me it isn't surprising that my first attempts at establishing a relationship with the opposite sex were a complete disaster. As a hormonal teenager I was full of enthusiasm but unfortunately totally inept which did little for my confidence. Getting a job at a Butlins holiday camp in Filey Yorkshire at the age of seventeen probably saved my life. It got me away from the claustrophobic environment at home and introduced me to the uninhibited world of free love of the late 60's. I was an innocent abroad, a hungry child let loose in a sweet shop for the first time and it's safe to say I made the most of it. I was lucky enough to find someone who was older and far more mature than I was, she was very patient to say the least and she took the time to fill in any gaps in my education. Butlins was my finishing school and although I may not have learned enough to get a distinction I certainly left there with much more confidence, a lot more life experienced a smile on my face and a spring in my step. Having tasted real freedom for the first time in my life there was no way I could go back to the way I had been living and it was only a matter of time before something had to give.

Against all odds I fell into a meaningful relationship. I can't say I fell in love because I didn't know what real love was as I had never experienced it, If anything I had fallen in love with

119

what I hoped love would feel like. What started out as a casual acquaintance developed into a friendship and it was out of that a relationship developed? Over the weeks we grew closer; I met her parents and visited her at the local school where she worked. I was spending more and more time with her during which time she moved house and I helped her move and decorate her new home but although I couldn't see it at the time the cracks were already beginning to show.

She was a few years older than me but that age gap was nothing compared to the vast differences in the other aspects of our lives. She was mature, educated and from a normal well balanced middle class family. I was immature uneducated and lacking in any kind of social skills. In short she was and had everything I ever wanted but a physical relationship no matter how strong couldn't hold it together indefinitely. We came from different worlds and looking back it could never be anymore than it was, but at the time it was a life line to normality that I didn't want to let go of.

It gave me a glimpse of a life that was alien to the one I was leading, totally removed from drink drugs, violence and mental illness. My happiness was short lived. The time I was spending away from home was triggering all sorts of alarm bells in my mother's mind. With her twisted selfish logic she knew she had to do something to put a stop to it and try to regain her control over me. She was no longer able to use violence and intimidation to get her way so the sharp edge of her tongue became her weapon of choice, and she put it to great use to inflict her poison and hatred. She would soon get her chance but it would come at a very high price for the both of us. Her venom finally triggered a violent and explosive outburst on my part as I vented all of the anger hatred and frustration that had built up over the years, as I tried to kill her. It coincided with the beginning of the end of the only meaningful relationship in my life. I felt totally empty and life just wasn't worth living anymore.

It's hard to put a finger on what actually caused this melt down. Looking back I think it was an accumulation of things that just came together and created a spark that lit the fuse that would ultimately blow my life apart. The happier I appeared the more bitter and twisted my mother became and the more biting and hurtful her remarks. That fateful day I had been staying at my girlfriend's house and returned home in a very happy mood which was a red rag to a bull as far as she was concerned. My happiness was short lived as she started with the usual barbed comments whose sole purpose was to intimidate, ridicule and hurt. She was succeeding until unwittingly she hit on a few simple words that while innocent in themselves were the trigger that unleashed years and years of pent up frustration, anger and hatred.

Her tirade was in full flow when she asked 'who did I think I was; trying to be better than anyone else'. Then all hell broke loose as I lost control and tried to kill her. To this day I still don't quite know what happened. I heard those words and it's as if they somehow reached deep down inside of me and I just snapped and the strangest thing happened. A red mist slowly descended in front of my eyes, like a red curtain it came down and turned my vision blood red. The next moment I was completely out of control screaming at my mother as I vented my anger. With my hands around her throat I started to strangle the life out of her. In the midst of that pain and anger I was intent on destroying the person who had caused me so much suffering. Yet something saved my mother's life and probably saved me from a lengthy stay in prison or a psychiatric hospital. At the time I didn't have chance to think about it, and it was many years later when age had given me a different perspective and a greater understanding I was able to detach from the emotion connected to that period in my life, and work through what had happened.

For a brief moment something broke through the anger and gave me the chance to see clearly what was about to happen if I continued to tighten my grip around my mother's throat. It went as quickly as it came but in that briefest of moments the spell was broken, I released my grip and spared her life.

Such was the intensity of the hatred I was feeling and the adrenalin overload surging through my body I began to destroy the house instead. I grabbed hold of the solid wooden door and literally ripped it off its hinges and threw it the length of the room before going outside and turning my attention to every window in the house. Having smashed everyone I could reach, I used anything I could find to hurl through each of the upstairs windows. By this time my anger and energy was totally spent and I collapsed in the garden as If I had been pole axed. In many ways history repeated itself that day. We both tried to take another's life and failed more by good luck than good management. We both escaped paying for our crimes in the eyes of the law, but the mental and emotional price I was about to pay was beyond anything I could have imagined even in my darkest moments of despair.

A mark in the sand

Leave your mark in the sand and it will be lost through the passing of time. Better to leave your mark in the hearts and minds of mankind, and through their deeds gain true immortality. For when we have gone all that will remain is the love that we have brought into this world.

Chapter Seventeen

One step from the edge

The day was warm and sunny. A brilliant blue sky provided a backdrop to the sun that felt warm on my face, yet the sight before me chilled me to the bone. Life had brought me to the edge of an abyss and at that moment I was unable to move. I was fearful of what lay before me and yet afraid of the darkness of depression that seemed to cling to me like a cold clammy sweat and affect every part of my life. Before me stood the imposing and frightening facade of the psychiatric hospital I had agreed to admit myself to for a series of tests and evaluations after my relatively young life nearly come to a premature end through depression, the misuse of drink and prescribed medication and a failed suicide attempt. Even the bright sunlight could do nothing to dispel the air of gloom and despair that seemed to permeate from the fabric of the building. It was as if the bricks and mortar had absorbed the pain suffering, and despair of the long forgotten inmates unfortunate enough to have lived and died within the walls of what was originally the Durham County Asylum.

Built on land between the villages of Fishburn and Sedgefield in 1855 the hospital initially consisted of a three story asylum built in the Elizabethan style with 300 beds for inmates, along with a chapel and superintendent's quarters. To keep pace with a growing need between 1875 and 1880, a major extension of the hospital was undertaken creating space for an extra 400 inmates.

It also had its own mortuary and cemetery within its grounds for those unfortunate souls who once committed to this place would never leave. With the changing attitudes towards mental health long stay hospitals began to close in the mid 70's which indirectly led to the onset of care in the community and the decision was made to close the hospital in 1996 after nearly 140 years. It's impossible to imagine what life was like for those unfortunate enough to be committed to that God forsaken place in years gone by. Some for no other reason than they were paupers, others deemed slow or of low intelligence, and children guilty of petty crime who would spend the rest of their lives within the walls of this institution. In some cases young unmarried mothers or women who simply suffered with pre-menstrual tension, and post-natal depression we interned there. There were even recorded cases of women who were committed by their husbands for no other reason than they were wilful and dared to question their husband's authority. For some of the inmates death would be their only release.

Fate would eventually provide macabre evidence that even in death there was no escape from the abuse of their rights and total disregard for their dignity. As it was being demolished the hospital gave up some of its gruesome secrets from its dark and inhuman past. During the demolition contractors discovered walled up rooms and corridors below ground. When they eventually broke through into these disused and forgotten basement tunnels and rooms they were horrified to discover numerous preserved body parts removed from inmates over the years. There are no records available to show what exactly was found or how many inmates were used in the name of research, but one must ask how many of the inmates went to their final resting place within the grounds of that institution broken in mind body and spirit.

If the building left me cold what happened next left me terrified and visibly shaken. As I stood outside of the gates I was approached by one of the patients who were obviously distressed and displaying some form of severe mental illness. In the grip of ignorance and fear the person I saw before me represented in my mind everything this dark depressing place stood for. I have never felt so afraid, lost or alone as I did in that moment, had I known what was to come I would have turned and ran as fast as I could and probably disappeared into the same darkness that claimed my mother's life. Much of my short stay in the hospital was a blur of boredom induced sleep interspersed by the staff waking patients for their meds, or by the harsh sounds of agitated patients that seem to reverberate around the rooms and corridors. Because I was a voluntary admission I was allowed come and go as I pleased with very few restrictions placed on me other than those created by routines and normal operating practices. I was also spared from having to endure the pain of electric shock therapy. Other patients weren't so fortunate and I quickly learnt to recognise the telltale signs once they had 'recovered' and returned to the communal areas. Quiet and subdued with slowness in speech, a near vacant expression in their eyes as if they were searching for something in their minds that was no longer there. Minds wiped clean of memories and in some case their identity.

I also became aware of the no go areas, the secure units where patients were detained who were a danger to themselves, and in some cases a danger to others. One of my overriding memories is the feeling that you were always being watched and if anything happened that was outside of the established routine, staff would appear out of nowhere and then disappear as quickly as they came.

When you are immersed in an environment of mental illness you can quickly begin to question your own sanity and with time lose perspective what normal behaviour is. The only bench mark you have is within your own mind, but sooner or later that will lose its grip on reality as long stay patients become institutionalised. I was there for a week and in that time I met patients that frightened me, people who inspired me and those who made me feel ashamed for wallowing in self-pity. Three people in particular stand out in my mind as a legacy of my time in that institution. An old lady in her eighties committed in her early teens for having a child out of wedlock and as such considered an 'unfit mother'. She became institutionalised decades before I was even born; the inside of the hospital was her home and the sum total of her life.

There was an elderly gentleman in the truest sense of the word. He was obviously well educated, extremely well spoken who bore the physical and psychological scars of the frontal lobotomy carried out to 'cure' his mental illness, but the person who helped me the most was the young man who made me feel ashamed for feeling sorry for myself. In the space of one short conversation he put my whole life into clear perspective. Whilst I never knew his name his story is etched into my memory and was literally the turning point in my life. Put into care as a child because his parents couldn't afford to look after him properly, they eventually had more children, but he was left in care. Did his problems start before or after he was put into care? I don't know but I will never forget the pain anger and confusion in his eyes when he spoke of being abandoned, or the self-inflicted scars on his arms and wrists through self-harming and attempted suicides.

After our conversation he walked out of the room and I never saw him again. With my head in my hands I sat and listened to his story over and over again in my mind and in that moment I knew my time in the hospital had come to an end. I took the time to collect my thoughts and my few possessions and then discharged myself the following day. As I stood outside the hospital that day I looked back one last time, the fear had gone to be replaced by a sense of sadness for those who were left behind. I also felt a sense of relief that I had come through the experience intact if battered and emotionally bruised. It allowed me to witness sadness and suffering on a scale that I could never have imagined, and more importantly it put my life up to that point into clear perspective. I took one last look, said a silent prayer of thanks, turned and slowly walked away. That was the point where I began to turn my life around and slowly begin my climb out of the pit of depression. Nearly fifty years down the line there are still days when I stumble, but now I'm always heading towards the light.

Some years later I returned to what I thought was the very same spot outside of the hospital as a way of putting down a mile maker to how far I had come from those dark days. The hospital was long gone but a few of the smaller out buildings remained scattered amongst the new business developments and a few of the mature trees still remained that had grown up in the shadow of the hospital. Although the landscape had completely changed I still felt a chill as a feeling of deep sadness swept over me. Instinctively I looked up to see if a cloud had briefly obscured the sun but the sky was clear and bright with not a cloud in sight. Over active imagination or a distant echo created by the residual energy of all of those lost souls who passed through its doors and who remain buried there. They say religion is for those who don't want to go to hell and spirituality is for those who have already been there. My life now is a spiritual journey in search or knowledge and understanding. Would I say that I have been to hell and back? Certainly not; but I was given the opportunity to stand at the edge of the abyss and given the choice to either fall into the darkness and be lost forever, or to come to the edge, fly and be all that I can be.

Out of the Darkness and into the Light

Slowly we emerge from the darkness and into the light; afraid and uncertain we pray the nightmare is over yet scared the pain may return. Wanting release from this uncertainty, we search for kindness in those who care enough to release us from the fear that holds us captive.

Need, fear and desperation separate us from that which we desire; life, repeating itself until new lessons are learnt from old experiences. Fragile confidence hides a love to share, yet trust, that cruel joke, keeps repeating never, never, never again.

Fear and despair are barren; worn like a mantle or a burden carried within filling our every thought. But now is the time to move beyond the limits of your own conditioning, and release the child of long ago, no longer a captive or victim to those who would hurt you. These faltering steps of forgiveness for others now require you to also forgive yourself and lay the burden down.

Love needs light to develop and grow. When we choose the light we give courage to others and permission to ourselves to let go of the past, accept the present, and embrace the future. In the knowledge that before we can receive love into our lives we must first let go of that which we have out grown, and create a place for that which we hope to become.

Chapter Eighteen

My years in the wilderness

I call the time between my stay in hospital in 1969 to when Reiki came into my life in 1999 as my wilderness years. The term may create a mental image of a barren landscape devoid of life or substance but the reality was just the opposite. This was a lengthy period in my life when I collected possessions to the point where my life was full to overflowing yet initially I had little appreciation for any of it. I married at the age of twenty three after meeting and knowing my future wife for about three months. Everyone was of the same opinion that the marriage would be lucky to last longer than the courtship, as it turned out we proved them wrong by nearly thirty years. Children growing up use their parents and immediate family as role models that hopefully provide them with a bench mark later in life as to how to be a husband, wife and a parent. I got married and started a family because that's what you are supposed to do at a certain age, and it was my way of escaping the life I had known. In all honesty for many years I was totally inept at being a husband and a father. My redeeming quality was that my heart was in the right place if nothing else.

My own role models were non-existent. No father figure from the age of five or six, and a mother who because of her mental illness spent more time in her own twilight zone than the real world. Put simply I didn't know how I was supposed to be a husband or a parent and it took many years before I was able to get a handle on both roles. During this time we started out with very little as a lot of people do, and slowly built a life together, moving several times until we were able to afford our own home, a car and nice possessions. We started a family, had two children a boy and a girl and adopted two of my sister's children, both boys, so that they would hopefully have a better start in life than my sister and I had. Again my heart was in the right place but my parenting skills left a great deal to be desired. I focussed a lot of time and energy on trying to be a father figure and eventually got there, but it never occurred to me just being a dad to my children was far more important than trying to be the 'perfect father'.

When we were first married my mother was still alive and she hated my wife on sight and did everything in her power to destroy our marriage in the same way she had tried with my sister and brothers marriages. This had nothing to do with her love for me or because she felt we were making a mistake. This was hatred pure and simple, and a demonstration of power and control. My mother was brought up to believe that violence was a legitimate means of control and imposing your will on others. In her life violence wasn't just accepted it was expected and when she was no longer able to impose her will with her fists she used the cutting edge of her tongue to inflict the damage and give vent to her anger and frustrations.

Eventually we moved away and I stopped going to visit her, not because I didn't care anymore but because of the damage my visits were doing to my family. She was content to live in dirt and squalor and such was the toxic atmosphere and the hatred, every time I returned home it seemed to cling to me and I was unbearable to live with for several days after.

I never allowed my children to go with me on those visits because I was ashamed and I wanted to protect them from their own grandmother. However one time my daughter who was three or four at the time was adamant she was going. The visit was as short as I could make it and when we returned home she described the scene to my wife in her own words. She said she had been to visit a witch in a dirty house that smelt awful and was very dark because the curtains were drawn to keep the daylight out. My daughter never asked to go again and my visits came to an end when after failing to get the response she wanted from attacking me or my wife, she turned her attention to our children, and at that point she broke my heart and our relationship was finally broken beyond repair. The next time I would see my mother she was laid in the mortuary as a result of suffering a major embolism. She had died doing what she enjoyed the most, drinking to still the nerves, quieten the voices and take the pain away. My brother couldn't face identifying her body so I said that I would go in his place. What struck me the most was how small she appeared and I knew I had done the right thing by sparing my brother the pain of seeing her lying there. Once again my heart was in the right place but broken into many pieces. It would stay that way until Reiki helped to put the pieces back together again.

Maybe it was from that point I began to change but change I did. We became foster parents as a result of adopting my sister's two boys. I would like to think I became a more loving husband and father, although it would be a long time before I was able to stop being so intense and relax more as a person. Somewhere around that time I realised that I needed to make up for lost time and start a caring offensive with my sole aim of making my family happy and letting them know each day that I loved them. All my wife had to say was she liked something for me to move heaven and earth to get it for her, the kids got everything I never had and we were still paying off the debt from one Xmas, when the next one was due to arrive. Unfortunately human nature being what it is I appeared to go from one extreme to the other, and in hindsight it must have been overpowering. At one point my wife said it felt like I was trying to buy her and the kids love and affection. If truth were known I probably was although I didn't realise it at the time.

I may not have been sure of when the changes began I have no doubts what so ever that they were taking place. I was growing up mentally, emotionally and most importantly spiritually and in a three-horse race it was my spiritual needs that were driving the other two forward. It was around this time that the major cracks began to appear in the important aspects of my life. My wife and I had grown apart, not intentionally but over the years we had grown into different people from the ones who had met and married so many years ago.

We now had different values, different beliefs and a different outlook on life. The children had grown, were becoming independent and in some cases leaving home. All of the ties that make a family strong were no longer there and the need for change was much stronger than the desire to hold things together. Some would say that the change when it came was too little too late and once a relationship goes beyond a certain point with the best will in the world you can't get it back to what it used to be. When that part of my life came to an end in 2000 even though I knew it was the best thing for all concerned it was still a very painful and stressful experience. My lasting regret from that part of my life is I wasn't the husband I could have been or the dad I should have been. Evidence if it was needed that no matter how far I have come I am still a work in progress and I still have so much to learn.

Homeward Journey

I have walked with wise men and listened to their truth spoken since time began. I have sat at the feet of teachers to receive their knowledge and understanding.

I have fought with warriors who embraced death in the fullness of life accepting that death is as much a part of life as the breath we take. I have listened to the peacemakers and learned of their love for life given up without regret for their fellow men.

In doing so I have regained the wonder of childhood seeing miracles in all things, yet with maturity I have gained the ability to love without judgment, accept without conditions and to give without regret. In letting go of that which I desired the most I gave up the fear of losing what I already had, for those things we fear and desire the most are within.

The path of learning must deliver us to our own darkness for this is where the greatest teacher patiently awaits our return.

Chapter Nineteen

When an old hurt becomes a new healing

The path of personal and spiritual development is never straight forward, and based on my own experience it's a path full of pot holes and pit falls. Delays and detours are in abundance; sufficient to test the patience of any would be saint. I'm neither saint nor sinner, perfect or imperfect; I am simply a work in progress as I struggle to get to know the stranger that lives my life. In the process I hope to become a better person.

No better than anyone else, simply a better person than I was yesterday, hopefully watched over by a universe who is guiding my faltering steps. The title of this chapter '*When an old hurt becomes a new healing*' reflects a personal need and desire to heal the past. I am a survivor of childhood abuse and neglect, and this particular spectre cast a long shadow over my life. There are no visible scars to see but the psychological scars I carry run very deep and are testament to a harsh painful childhood and the suffering inflicted by those who should have loved and cared for me. Healing is neither magical nor miraculous it's a process made possible through the power of knowledge and understanding. A process that raises our awareness, at the same time bringing a deeper understanding, of who and what we are, the events and circumstances that helped create the person we have become without the need for blame or self-recrimination.

As strange as it may seem the healing brought about by the writing of this book has helped me to acknowledge a debt of gratitude to the person responsible for the damaged caused in my childhood and formative years. That person was my mother. I have long since forgiven her for what happened but as yet I can't in all honesty say that I love her which in itself is evidence I still have a way to go on this particular leg of my journey. I was only able to forgive when I began to replace my anger and hatred with knowledge and understanding. Putting blame and judgement to one side I forced myself to detach from the emotions I was feeling and asked the question 'If I am this person who and what

142

made me this way'. I began to educate myself as to what happened and why, and the more I learnt the more compassion I felt for the person who had caused so much trauma in my life. I gained both understanding and perspective that enabled me to see her in a completely different light. Her childhood was far worse than anything I had experienced, she suffered the effects of an extremely violent father and a mother's ignorance that left her physically scarred and mentally and emotionally traumatised. As a result she was diagnosed with manic depression and a personality disorder presented in violent outbursts that were destructive and dangerous to herself and anyone around her. Prescribed medication and alcohol became her addiction later in life and was a contributing factor to her death at a relatively early age.

In writing this book I offer no solutions to anyone's problems other than my own. What worked for me may not work for you the reader. If you can relate to my experiences but need professional help to heal and let go of the past then you owe it to yourself to get all the help you can. Personal development should never be considered a substitute for professional help or seen as an easy option, its neither and all development work must have a solid stable foundation on which to build if it is to last and stand the test of time. You have a personal responsibility and a duty of care to yourself to ensure the healing you require takes place, and there comes a point in all healing modalities where the patient must reclaim their power, take personal responsibility and invest in their own health and wellbeing.

My thoughts are simply that, my thoughts that have been formed by my life experience and a desire to know myself, which I believe is the beginning of all true knowledge and understanding, and the power by which we heal ourselves. If children are the consequences of our actions and the effect of what we do becomes the legacy they must learn to live with, I ask the forgiveness of my own children, who I feel I failed as a father in those dark days when I knew no better. Through the desire to learn and understand I have been able to call a truce and make peace with my past. In doing so I can use the strength and courage gained through adversity to draw a line in the sand and accept the consequences of my own actions and the person I have become.

Progress can be a long and winding road

Progress is never straight forward; it's a process that is both incremental and directional made up of small faltering steps. A journey that is more often than not full of twists and turns, dead ends and delays. Where moments of clarity and clear thinking provide us with meaningful purpose and direction during those times when we may lose our footing, stumble and fall.

The clarity we seek often eludes us as confusion draws in to cloud our vision. A fog where all manner of fears and uncertainties hide, waiting to trip and ensnare the unsuspecting traveller. Progress can be slow and laboured as uncertainty becomes our travelling companion; the yellow brick road that would give us direction is obscured and overgrown and we are forced to break new ground and old beliefs in equal measure.

When we appear to lose our way this serves only to help us find our true path, a wrong direction is nothing more than a foot misplaced. It provides perspective and a point of reference to our development, the experience of failure is a gift that provides purpose and meaning to our successes no matter how small they may be.

A long and winding road; a journey to revisit the past, not to dwell there but to help us see how far we have come. Mile markers may measure our progress but development is neither orderly nor predetermined, it is often random taking us by surprise when we least expect it. Progress is a process, our destination is no further than the next faltering footstep that takes us ever forward.

Chapter Twenty

The first step to healing yourself is to recognise
who and what caused your illness

A fear once spoken breaks the spell and when faced loses
its power to control. The victim of abuse and neglect begins to
talk openly about a part of their life that was once so painful. A
time of pain and suffering for the child; but with age comes a
growing burden of guilt for whom, and what they have become.
Evil people never feel guilty in the same way the righteous do;
guilt is a self-inflicted punishment of the good for mistakes
made, real or imaginary. Mistakes made not from conscious

choice but by conditioning so intense it has the power to deform and scar whatever it touches. In many ways guilt is the parting gift of the abuser for they have created the victim and the belief in failure they hold to be true. This legacy that has the power to corrupt long after the physical abuse has ended. Guilt is a self-imposed sentence, and the victim will seek to punish themselves long after the abuser has gone.

A mistake is a lesson in the making, not a life sentence of self-inflicted punishment. Nor should it be motivation for a continual repayment of a debt that in reality was never owed. To heal oneself we need to find it in our hearts to forgive the abuser to secure our release from the past. The aim is not to condone but to recognise their role as co-creators in our mistakes. We must also find it in our hearts to forgive ourselves for until we do we are literally carrying the burden of guilt and will remain the victim of circumstances long past, and guilt will continue to inflict pain and suffering that is neither deserved nor required. Emotional pain is symptomatic of guilt and the more chronic the pain the more deep seated the guilt that seeks expression and acknowledgement before it can be released and healing of oneself can take place.

May the spirit of creation grant you the wisdom of knowledge and understanding? At every step of the way give thanks for the blessings you receive through its love and kindness. Let your actions cherish and respect all things, the

148

wonders of nature, and the magic of its creation. Walk softly lest you scar the earth with your passing and look kindly upon the beauty that lies before you.

Find the courage to be all that you can be whilst respecting the needs and desires of others. At all times try to live in peace with mankind no matter what their colour or creed, honour their beliefs as you do your own. Tomorrow is neither promised nor certain; don't waste it by regretting the past or fearing the future. Live your life to the full doing only what you can then let go of rest safe in the knowledge you have done your best.

Chapter Twenty-One

The path of learning is littered with pitfalls and stumbling
blocks

Reiki was a part of my life long before I knew it existed. It
ensured a lady got home safely on that cold dark night I stood in
the shadows and saw nothing but a victim to my own selfish
needs. It saved my mother's life in a moment of clarity that
stopped me from killing her. It intervened to save my life when I
tried to commit suicide and end it all. A journey that unbeknown
to me had yet to begin. Little did I know the time would come

when without knowing its name or understanding why, I would searched for it and invite it into my life.

Softly it entered to help bring about changes that left me in awe of its power, its knowledge and understanding to unfold. Never against my will; leading me out of the darkness discovering new ways and understanding that would eventually set me free. With each new opportunity I was given the chance to break new ground and old beliefs in equal measure. It's a journey we can all take. A path littered with stepping stones and stumbling blocks, a journey during which we are student and teacher, a seeker of truth and the giver of wisdom. Each step gifts us the opportunity to seek out the knowledge and understanding we are searching for. Where our foot falls doesn't matter for the lessons to be learned and the truths to be discovered are already within, our journey merely provides the experiences necessary to discover them. Our destination is a state of mind; its purpose to help us discover our true identity, and be one with all things.

The Pilgrim's way

I am a wayward pilgrim on a journey to God knows where. I find comfort in the past and what's gone before, yet I lack direction or destination, forever tripping over the doubts and fears that cause me to stumble and fall, heavy with the burden of guilt and regret, weary from the struggle yet unable to set it down. Fear and uncertainty are my constant companions,

152

their voices loud and mocking at every turn. Overwhelmed and confused I look to others to provide direction with each faltering step taking me closer to a destination yet unknown.

I seek to collect my troubled thoughts from the confusion that surrounds me. In answer to my prayer comes the realisation it's my struggles that have brought me to this moment of realisation. Suffering and resistance walk hand in hand; the more I blindly struggle the greater the fear and despair, and the more frightening my experience becomes.

When I stumbled and fell it was because I had ignored the voice of reason. In my haste I had forgotten that there is a time for all things. A time to struggle and overcome and a time to rest and reflect on how far we have travelled. The road lies before us but it's our thoughts, beliefs and actions that help create the landscape that we experience as life.

Taking my first faltering steps on this new path of discovery I cautiously searched for wisdom within and begins to look anew at a world with eyes of wonder and joy. Like the prodigal son returning home from a journey of self-discovery I can see how far I have travelled and the progress I have made. It's the journey that gifts us the opportunity to learn and discover who we really are. The moment we journey within for the answers we seek we are no longer lost or alone.

Now I view all things with love and compassion and in letting go of judgment of myself and attachment to all I have outgrown, I have discovered within myself a true purpose and meaning and have begun my journey home.

Chapter Twenty-Two

―――――◆◆◆――――――

I came to the edge ... and I flew .... eventually

―――――◆◆◆――――――

One of the greatest barriers for anyone to overcome on a journey of personal development is their lack confidence and self-doubt. I'm frequently asked 'what if I get it wrong or don't do it properly'. To answer this we must first ask the question 'how do we learn to do anything'? Learning is a process of trial and error; regardless of the subject matter the process is basically the same. We observe, we copy, practice and adjust until we get the result we want. Any level of proficiency has been achieved using this same process; from learning to walk to mastering a particular skill or ability, the principle remains the same. The old adage 'we learn by our mistakes' is only partly true. What is closer to the mark is we have the opportunity to learn by our mistakes, for not everyone wants to learn this way. Most of us if we were truthful don't want to make mistakes.

Mistakes can be embarrassing, making us feel inadequate and question our self-worth. Learning by mistakes is a rule we would prefer to apply to others, so we can get it right first time, every time. This desire to learn without making mistakes is neither practical nor supportive of our need to develop and grow. Getting something right by accident teaches us nothing for we tend to celebrate our successes and scrutinise our failures. Development requires perspective that comes through knowledge and understanding. We learn by observing others, copying them until our actions become established with practice.

We pretend to be something we think we are not until we become the thing we desire. A small child taking its first faltering steps; is a beautiful example of the learning process in action. Determination stubbornness, uncertainty and frustration as the child slowly master the ability to stand and walk alone. Physical strength is developed along with balance and co-ordination. Confidence grows with practice as the ability becomes second nature and we no longer have to think about what we are doing. Education asks us to release our grip on reality. Change can be uncomfortable; any new experience forces us to leave our comfort zone and step into the unknown. Learning a new skill or ability challenges what we accept to be true, and the perceptions we hold about ourselves.

But what if you get it wrong? So what; it's not the end of the world. We get it wrong so that we are given the opportunity to get it right next time and learn from the process. When you know better do better, it's that simple. We develop a greater level of knowledge and understanding of our ability and our connection to the world. We study and learn and in the process we try to emulate our teachers. We practice and pretend to be the thing we think we are not until it dawns on us that practice has evolved to become experience, we have grown into the thing we aspired to be. Come to the edge! It's unsafe! Come to the edge! I may fall! Come to the edge! I came to the edge, you pushed me and I flew.....eventually.

Normality isn't all it's cracked up to be

Normality is a great illusion that has the power to hold us secure. What we perceive as normal is simply a collection of beliefs, stereotypes and fears that we use as protection against the great unknown and those who appear strange and different. Normality demands that we fit in at all costs. It requires us to stifle our curiosity and sacrifice our free spirit at the altar of conformity. Normality seeks to control and subdue those who would dare to be different and ask 'what if'.

To be normal is the dream of those who want nothing more than to blend in, who have no desire to be different or stand out from the crowd. To them normality is the drug of choice, the sedative that subdues the spirit and disempower the mind that would otherwise seek answers found only in new experiences.

Normality requires our acceptance and obedience for without it, it is powerless. In awaking from the dream of mediocrity we see it for what it is in the light of knowledge and understanding. Awareness is the gateway that leads to the unknown, beyond the limitations set by tradition, custom and formality. In the unknown we once feared we find the space for self-acceptance and self-expression and the freedom to be all that we can be.

Chapter Twenty-Three

"Spiritual" myths we need to challenge

An urban myth is defined as 'a story told as if it actually happened'. A story told in such a way that the listener accepts it as a matter of fact. Repeat something often enough and people will begin to accept it as if it were true. Even a lie told often enough will achieve the credibility of fact if enough people buy into it. Social myths can be amusing but those associated with Reiki and its perceived spirituality if allowed to go unchecked have the potential to create confusion, undermine credibility, yet urban myths are nothing new. Myths and mankind have always walked hand in hand. Early in my Reiki career I was told in no uncertain terms by a Reiki Master that I should never give Reiki to anyone who was seated with their legs crossed as this position has the power to stop the energy flowing. Really! Initially I accepted everything I was taught and never thought to challenge or question these ''facts''. When my own practice began to provide experiential evidence to disprove these myths I began to question everything. To strip away the myths and misconceptions, the old wives tales that through repetition and blind obedience had taken on the persona of spiritual truths.

Sometimes we must unlearn the lies in order to reclaim the truth substantiated by evidence and proof. This means we must get back to basics and unpick the story and separate the fact from fiction. When Reiki is used as a form of personal development, you need to ask yourself the question ''are you worth the effort necessary to transform your life''. To me Reiki is an expression of unconditional love and creative energy that at the last count was responsible for all life on earth, and the creation of billions of galaxies, so I can't quite get my head around the 'spiritual fact' that simply crossing our legs renders this creative force powerless. I've been told many such myths by teachers and practitioners alike. Instructions given as gospel yet never once supported by research based evidence. They believed Reiki to be a spiritual discipline and such stories were considered spiritual by association, I was simply expected to accept them without questioning their validity. My experiences as a Reiki Master teacher have proven these myths and misconceptions to be unfounded and unsubstantiated.

160

Of all the Reiki myths I have encountered there is one that stands head and shoulders above the rest. A myth that is so misleading, unhelpful and unhealthy, it undermines the principles of Reiki when sold and promoted as a miracle cure that heals everyone it touches. It isn't, and it can't, because it doesn't have the authority to do so. To do so would go against the principles of unconditional love and free will. Both are sacrosanct along with other spiritual laws that provide the structure and framework to creation. By the nature of its existence it must adhere to the forces that were instrumental in its creation; the created can never be greater than its creator, exist beyond its grace and control, or act arbitrarily outside of its laws.

If we clear away all of the uncertainty and confusion we discover a solid foundation and the fundamental precept of 'the only person we can heal is ourselves'. With these eight simple words comes the implication and confirmation that the healing process can't take place in our absence, or be forced upon us. Change is inevitable but personal development requires choices to be made, and as hard as it may seem, not everyone who is ill knowingly wants to be made well. Some have claimed their illness as their own; it gives a sense purpose and identity, and as such Reiki cannot and will not heal that person against their will. Knowledge and understanding are the true physicians of healing who provide the opportunity to learn and grow, to become receptive to the physical and spiritual help available to them. In doing so they can if they so wish, develop in mind body and spirit, eventually reaching the point where they take personal responsibility, and play an active role in their own healing.

This is truth demonstrated and the true purpose of all healing modalities. Working to the persons highest good, and the realisation all healing ultimately comes through knowledge and understanding. Without it healing of any description is impossible. Even the miraculous must adhere to this same principle. What is perceived as a miracle is nothing more than an event that exists outside the limits of our current knowledge and understanding. Once we expand that knowledge and understanding what was once perceived as a miracle becomes a skill, a spirit based technology to be used time and time again to improve the quality of life, to empower the individual, and to heal illnesses and disease. Any time we come across questionable must do's and contra-indicators that fly in the face of common sense and logic we should hold them up to the light of scrutiny and test their substance, credibility, and truth. We must be careful not to confuse spiritual integrity with the man made historical dogma that evolves over time with any discipline. We should always ask if these stories are based on a human belief or a spiritual truth. If they resonate with you then be true to yourself whatever that may be, if not let them go and continue on your personal journey of discovery.

The myth may remain constant but the same can't be said about our desire for knowledge and understanding. There was once a myth that the earth was flat; it was said if you sailed into the horizon you would fall off the edge of the world and into oblivion. Every time this myth was repeated it gained credibility until only those who were brave enough dared to challenge those beliefs and fears. In doing so they helped expanded our physical and spiritual horizons and bring us out of the dark ages of superstition and mythology and into the dawning light of knowledge and understanding.

A Pilgrim's prayer

As I struggle to develop and grow, judge me not on the progress made, but on who and what I can become. Help me to realise comparisons are meaningless when I consider what I have achieved and how far I have come.

We are all on a journey of personal discovery, and even though I may stumble and fall I pray for the strength and courage to help my fellow traveller on the road to their fulfilment.

Above all else bless me with knowledge and understanding for with it I am at peace with myself and the universe that gifts me life. In understanding I have found peace and purpose to life and with it the knowledge that the universe is guiding my faltering steps.

Chapter Twenty-Four

Stuff before it was stuff with labels attached to it

Reiki as we know and understand it was introduced to the world in the late 1800's, and by definition a 'universal energy' for over a hundred years known as Reiki. It's important we understand Reiki is just a name, a label that's been attached to it in order to try and define the infinite, and give ourselves a point of reference. Since the universe didn't just appear at the end of the 19th century it's reasonable to assume this energy has been around for a much longer period, and expressed in many ways before Dr Usui rediscovered it and gave it a name that has meaning and relevance to his language and culture.

If he had been called Black Elk, a North American first nation Shaman or medicine man, the name attributed to the energy, the values and teachings would have reflected his particular culture and belief system with all of the spiritualism and symbolism that goes with it. We can see from this Reiki is a 'brand name' for what is a very generic universal product. A label attached to something much bigger, more dynamic and more powerful, that's infinite in size duration and meaning. Labels have their uses but when attached to people the wearer will either live up or down to the value conveyed. The label takes on an identity all of its own and the person becomes invisible. We look at the label and make judgements based on what it says. This is who or what it is' and we no longer look beyond the limitations that measurement imposes to seek out its true nature or meaning.

If as the story says Dr Usui 'rediscovered' Reiki then we should ask the question was this infinite energy lost in Japan at that point in time, misplaced or were they simply overlooking what had always been there. To put the hundred and thirty year Reiki history into context it may help to consider some scientific and biblical numbers available to us. Science informs us that the universe is approximately fourteen billion years old. The earth was four and a half million years in the making, populated by 'modern' Homo sapiens in their many forms for the last two hundred thousand years. This they say was part of the universe's and mankind ongoing evolutionary process, a process they add, free from divine purpose or intervention. The biblical timeline is much shorter but no less confusing. We are told a creator who existed before time had meaning.

Through his infinite power and wisdom created the universe and everything in it over a period of six days. On the seventh day he rested to admire his handy work, and was, we are told, impressed with what he had created. Obviously, there is a real conflict between these two versions of events but we must remember that nothing is set in stone and both science and religion are defined and directed by their own evolutionary processes.

There was a time in mankind's history when the churches ruled supreme and were too powerful to be challenged. The biblical records available at the time were presented literally as gospel to be accepted without question as the factual and truthful word of God the creator. Those who couldn't or wouldn't accept this version of events risked punishment at hands of the religious establishment. The ascent of science provided both the evidence and power to challenge the might of the church and the validity of its written word. What was once viewed as sacrosanct is now accepted by many clergy and theologians as a spiritual story that shouldn't be taken literally as the obvious flaws and inaccuracies undermine the spiritual values it promotes. Science has fared no better as one scientific model after another has been promoted only to be replaced as contemporary knowledge and understanding changes the way we think the universe works. The technological advances provided by science come at a heavy price with mother earth having to suffer the consequences and pick up the bill like a dutiful parent for the actions of her wayward children. Both science and religion are the self-proclaimed saviours of mankind yet both have failed. Science extols its own virtues writing off pollution and toxic waste as an acceptable price for progress, whilst religion takes up its usual position on the moral high ground blaming anything that can't be explained through common sense, logic or reasoning on God's will, thus ensuring the buck never stops with them.

So if Reiki is neither science nor religion what was it before we attached the Reiki label to it? Religion isn't the same as spirituality and it has to be said that God however you wish define him/her/it/them isn't the same as spirituality. For thousands of years in diverse cultures around the world, inspired spiritual teachers such as the Buddha, Jesus, Confucius proposed life changing views that were based on the attainment of consciousness. In laymen's terms the acquisition and application of knowledge and understanding in their everyday life?

They taught there is a reality that lies beyond the limitations of our physical senses. We can experience the physical world, but beyond the reach of the five senses lays an invisible realm of infinite possibility that responds to our thoughts, beliefs and actions. The key to unlocking its potential is consciousness, or the acquisition and application of knowledge and understanding. Go within, the teachers said and you will find the true source of everything: including your own greatness through the realisation of your true self. Today the teachers of quantum physics are repeating a similar message, the language is different but the message remains the same. These ancient teachers offered something far more radical than a disempowering belief in a detached higher power. An alternative way of viewing reality that begins with inner wisdom, personal responsibility, and access to infinite knowledge and understanding.

The irony is these teachers were in their own way breaking new ground and old beliefs in equal measure. Spiritual truths to be tested to see if they were valid, through practice a truth demonstrated. Offering this new way of achieving knowledge and understanding to those who would listen, asking them to take the responsibility of applying it to their own lives in order to raise their level of awareness and the life changing benefits this would bring. The lessons presented to the world thousands of years ago contain three spiritual elements that will resonate within every modern day seeker of truth. Firstly, there is an unseen or invisible energy force or reality that is the source of all matter or things visible. This invisible force can be known and understood through the raising of our own awareness. And finally, there is intelligence, a creative power embedded in the cosmos that links, illuminates and animates everything within it.

Labels no matter how descriptive are just a momentary footnote on an infinite timeline whose origins can't be explained in isolation by either science or religion. The answer is to be found in the middle ground of spirituality. When science can finally accept it doesn't own the monopoly on man's development. A time when we are willing to look beyond the labels of Gods regardless of denomination with the restriction of measurement those labels impose, surrendering the belief that they alone hold the power and responsibility for mankind's salvation. Knowledge and understanding is the basis of all personal development and the healing it brings, for without it healing in the truest sense of the word would be impossible. A process of truth demonstrated where a change in perception is a prerequisite to the healing of the condition. Without knowledge and the understanding it brings we remain ignorant to the underlying causes of all problems, issues, illnesses and diseases hiding in the darkness of ignorance and fear.

A name is just a Label

A name is just a label; do the names we use describe us, or help create the person we become. What do you see when you look at me, does the name you give me reflect the true nature within?

A name is a label we place on one another. A mark of identity, that shows the world who we are. Do these labels do us justice and reflect the truth behind the mirrors image, an image that we alone can see.

We are so much more than the labels we wear. Do these names come from a place of love, or fear? Do they tell the whole truth, or are they limited by what we hold to be true?

When we look at others what qualities do we see? Can we see the real person behind the appearance life has given them? Can we look through the eyes of the heart and see their true worth, or do we look no further than the differences made real by our own ignorance and fear.

Can we find it within ourselves to look beyond the labels we once used? Can we learn to see into a heart and soul that shares the same desire for love and life; the need to be accept for whom they are, all they can become?

As we begin to heal ourselves the need for labels will fall away, replaced by truth, knowledge and understanding. Be gentle in your judgement and considerate in all that you do for the labels you place on others will be placed on you.

171

Chapter Twenty-Five

The truth is in there somewhere ....

all we have to do is find it

As a qualified trainer and Reiki teacher delivering personal development training programmes, part of my educational and vocational remit is to train students who want to learn and hopefully for some, one day become teachers and trainers themselves. This requires an understanding of accepted academic principles and teaching practices, coupled with the ability and experience to deliver sometimes complex subjects in a way that makes it easy for the student to understand. These subjects by their very nature can be very difficult to comprehend, hard to accept and even harder to substantiate. I find an open community of enquiry is an excellent teaching model as it works on the premise that there are no definitive right or wrong answers, just differing points of view. This often leads to a discussion on a wide range of related subjects such as religion, spirituality, reincarnation life after death and their relevance to life in general, and the study of Reiki. If we are serious in our desire to gain knowledge and understanding in our pursuit of personal development, Reiki, spirituality or any other subject can't be considered in isolation.

We must when necessary, be willing to discuss the physical and spiritual framework wherein life death, healing and dis-ease coexist, their implications and the questions in the minds of the student. As educators we must be willing to examine all avenues of thought until we reach a place of objectivity, even if it forces us to step outside of our own academic and philosophical comfort zone. To be objective it's vital that we move away from hearsay, supposition and folklore, and provide were possible research based data, as well as experiential evidence to back up what we teach. Students must trust the knowledge they acquire, they must trust their teachers and mentors, and as a teacher I have a responsibility to ensure reliability, validity and authenticity in all that I do.

This doesn't mean we spoon feed the student and provide all of the answers. This approach dis-empowers them and creates lazy students. We have a duty to empower the student to think, but not necessarily what to think. This requires us to facilitate learning and stimulate the students desire to seek out knowledge and understanding for themselves, and through this process take ownership for their learning and personal development.

To ensure this we must where necessary, authenticate the subject matter in order to validate our teachings, be prepared to analyse and critically evaluate the findings, and if necessary be willing to change our views, beliefs and teaching practice if the evidence and facts demand it. No matter how well intentioned or spiritual it may appear tradition should never be at the expense of knowledge and understanding or used to justify the perpetuation of ideas or ideals that lack substance or credibility. Learning requires where ever possible, we deal in factual based knowledge. To do so we must look beyond the myths and legends to find the truth, no matter how strange it may first appear or how uncomfortable it makes us feel, as we move out of our comfort zone and into the realms of the unknown. Knowledge and understanding are intrinsic to our personal development and growth, and this always lies beyond what we already know and accept as fact. Education asks us to release our grip on reality and embrace the unknown.

The miraculous is anything that exits beyond our current sphere of perception or awareness, and as a species we sometimes struggle to come to grips with our world and understand the nature of events it presents to us. We look to make sense of anything that doesn't appear to fit the norm or challenges our beliefs, assumptions or social values. To allay our fears and ensuing confusion, we look for ways to reinforce our existing beliefs and make sense of the events in our lives. In many ways we attempt to discern patterns or purpose in seemingly unconnected events in order to better grasp their significance. We say Reiki has changed my life, but it's we who have changed. What we perceive to be Reiki may provide inspiration and direction but we have ultimate responsibility to live our lives in the way we choose. Reiki is neither intrusive nor dictatorial; it has neither the power nor the desire to override our free will and freedom of choice. Unfortunately a belief once established filters out all incoming information and reject anything that challenges its existence. We will do everything in our power to justify our beliefs or prejudices even if they fly in the face of all common sense, logic and reasoning.

A problem teachers can face is their own objectivity in their chosen field of study, and this can be compounded when their personal experiences impact on their research in either a positive or negative way. Some would go so far as to deny the possibility of objective study, and argue that all research is inescapably subjective; others maintain the that the proper quest of social scientific research is objective truth in itself. In light of the esoteric nature of the subject matter, my own search for objective truth demands that I ask the question; if our beliefs are a matter of choice and experiences are a matter of fact, how can we reconcile our Reiki experiences no matter how factual they may be, when they appear to contradict existing scientific thinking?

Reiki teachers and practitioners alike are adamant that Reiki works, yet medical science says there is no scientific proof to substantiate this, and perceived results are merely due to mind over matter, the placebo effect. This is the same placebo effect that helps medication work in the form of a belief in the doctor and the medication to make us well again. The mind is over matter logistically figuratively and intellectually, for the mind sets the parameters and the body conforms to the directives it receives.

To be able to answer this question I need to examine the aspects of experience, reasoning and research. Analyse the nature of our belief system and critically evaluate the source and validity of those beliefs. How they under pin our experiences, and to understand what beliefs and experiences are. The dictionary defines a belief as a feeling of certainty and when we examine the origins of these feelings of certainty we discover that they can be learned in the same way we acquire any other form of information. They can come from re-enforced peer group or social pressure that determines what is 'right' or socially acceptable, or be hereditary, in as much as it becomes a family or social tradition passed down from generation to generation. Experience is direct personal participation or observation in or of an event, and so we begin to realise that a sustained or firmly held belief may well be supported or underpinned by experiences that validate the belief. If, as in the original question we have no personal experience of Reiki or any other related esoteric phenomena, we will find it difficult if not impossible to believe in the existence of anything that is beyond the limits of the physical senses.

If however an element of doubt is introduced into the belief/experience loop we may begin to question the established belief which is fundamental to personal development and a greater level of knowledge and understanding. A simple example was our belief in Santa Clause; as children we believed Santa Clause was real because of the experiences and references that supported that belief. Our parents told us he was real, and on Xmas morning the presents we received provided in our mind absolute proof that he existed. It was only when we began to question our parents and the existence of a Santa Clause did we eventually accept that he didn't actually exist in the way we thought he did. This particular belief is sustained be it for 'all the right reasons' by misinformation or lies on the part of parents and the lack of knowledge and understanding on the part of children.

Those who teach us can only do so based on what they themselves have learnt. The beliefs and values given to us by our parents and/or society are usually to control us, keep us safe and to stop us being disappointed in life. What we believe in usually determines both attitude and behaviour towards oneself and towards others. We come into the world pristine but very quickly pick up and accept the views, beliefs and expectations of society and the authority figures around us. A lot of baggage we carry in the form of attitudes, beliefs and values are inherited or accepted initially without a great deal of thought for their origins or authenticity. How many of us during our Reiki training accepted what our Reiki Master told us without question, Reiki being such a 'spiritual' discipline what we are told must be true. Yet a search for objectivity asks that we question the old and the new in equal measure in order to search out the truth.

Reason is the faculty of rational argument, deduction and judgement. Our ability to reason is defined by our intellectual capacity and to a greater degree our collective knowledge and understanding. Reason is the power which enables the mind to grasp reality but as we are beginning to realise what we think and believe effects our perception of that reality.

Rational argument, deduction and judgement demand the consideration and evaluation of all evidence new and old, rather than rejection or dismissal based on personal dogma, social conditioning or even a negative subjective experience. The

179

ability to reason requires us to understand the concept of reasoning and be willing to open our minds enough to accept new truths, which is the basis of all personal, educational and social development, and eventually healing through the acquisition and application of knowledge and understanding. You may say that our ability to think is an integral part of the reasoning process, but thinking alone won't necessarily bring about a quantum leap in understanding or acceptance of a new idea or belief. Thinking is a matter of consciously considering what already exists in our minds, which is the sum total of what we have experienced in the past. So the act of thinking appears to be a mental exercise that brings our memories or established beliefs to bear upon the present moment or new information we are being asked to consider. Objectivity requires an open mind free from the filter of preconceived ideas and beliefs.

To answer my original question we also need to examine the development of the science that says Reiki can't work. The science that defines our world, its strengths, and its limitations in dealing with anything that falls outside the parameters of our physical senses. Our world is defined by our five senses; our sense of sight, touch, hearing, smell and taste inform us what is real in our physical environment, it's the physiological and neurological antenna that enables us to navigate the hazards of everyday life. Our senses are hard wired to our brain; disconnect them and they are unable to provide us with the neurological and electrical impulses (information) it needs. We see, feel, hear, smell and taste more with our Brain than we do with the external organs that act as a conduit. What you believe to be real is nothing more than electrical impulses to and from your brain. Science no matter how well established is still only a work in progress no more than a few hundred years old, its credibility no greater than its best results and its reputation no better than its worse mistake. All new discoveries go through the same evolutionary process of indifference, scepticism, hostility and resistance, before finally being accepted as the norm by its peers. History is littered with references to visionaries such as Tesla, Bell, Edison, Newton and Einstein, being ridiculed and derided because they dared to challenge the accepted beliefs with new truths.

Historically our knowledge and understanding of the world come from the sciences and the church. The maxim of science is: *Accept no one's word for it,* and the church's word is *gospel that must be accepted without question* yet we take science and the church's word on reality and morality without question. It is said that science and religion are mighty because they are right, but in our search for objectivity should we not ask ourselves; is science and religion right because they are mighty?

The responsibility for our education rests solely with us and we shouldn't negate or relinquish that responsibility to others no matter how authoritative they may appear. Before we blindly accept social and religious dogma as our own we should first carefully consider the words of the German philosopher Johann Most. 'The more man clings to religious dogma, the more he believes. The more he believes, the less he knows. The less he knows the more stupid he is. The more stupid, the easier he can be governed'. Sir Isaac Newton's eighteenth century scientific model of the world is still the basis for some of our existing beliefs of who we are and what is possible. Even though we have entered the twenty first century of quantum entanglement, physics and super string theories which mathematically prove we live in a multi-dimensional world that can include a spirit dimension, some still hold the belief that if a thing can't be seen, if it can't be scientifically measured and duplicated in a laboratory then it can't exist.

There are parts of the religious and political establishment that invest heavily in the perpetuation of the doctrine that healing of the body and spirit is the sole jurisdiction of the medical profession and the church. Disciplines such as Reiki are at best misguided and at worst dangerous or evil in the guise of good intentions. Yet thanks to the emergence of quantum physics and quantum mechanics over the last hundred and fifty years, science has come to accept a universe made up solely of energy, the vast majority of which lies beyond the range of our physical senses. A universe we are a part of what is energy in nature, defined by and through vibration that exists everywhere all of the time. Thus recognising and accepting that matter in the form of solid objects as we understand it doesn't exist in the way we think it does.

Through the study of quantum physics and quantum mechanics it has been proven mathematically, which is a prerequisite for scientific validation, quantum wave and particles allows for separate dimensions or realities to exist here and now, sharing our space separated only by the shape and vibration of their energetic blueprint. Could it be possible that the source of Reiki energy owes more to quantum physics than it does to eastern mythology and spirituality in the way we have been led to believe.

If disciplines like Reiki exist, and I believe that it does surely it's more important to discover its true point of origin than to simply accept without question, and pay lip service to tradition. If we required further proof of the collaboration between science and religion to influence and control what we think and believe, we need look no further than a reported conversation between eminent physicist Professor Stephen Hawking and Pope John Paul the second, during which the Pope said ''I do not care what you do with your scientific research just so long as you do not encroach on my subject of the spirit world and life after death''. If true this is a clear indication of religion and science collaborating to suppress investigation and validation of realities that lie outside of the accepted religious domain. When challenged on this matter, the Royal Society stated that its policy which dates back to the 17th century, agreed with the church never to trespass into the subject of life after death. If quantum physics is correct and other dimensions exist then is it possible there is a spirit dimension by definition, nondenominational.

Neither heaven nor hell, and free from all religious dogma, a spirit dimension that we all automatically transcend to at the end of this physical life. Is it also possible that the church has known this fact for many years? The suppression of uncomfortable ideas may be common in religion and politics, but it is not the path to knowledge and understanding, it has no place in the pursuit of science, education or learning.

One thing is certain those who have experienced Reiki believe no further proof is required and through it, their understanding of the healing process has changed the way they think about life in general, and the lessons to be learnt. Those who haven't, remain steadfastly sceptical and dismissive. The volume of evidence supporting disciplines such as Reiki will grow steadily as the boundaries of science are pushed further aside to uncover the truth hidden by a lack of knowledge and understanding on our part, or a desire to control what we think and believe by elements of the church, scientific and political establishment. Knowledge is power and those who control and disseminate that knowledge ultimately control the direction of society's development and growth.

Legitimate and sustainable scientific research has historically been discredited along with the character and reputations of those who would challenge the status quo and introduce new truths into the public domain. We must ask ourselves what could generate such fear and a desire to suppress the truth. The answer is that those who suppress truth do so in order to suppress their own fear and maintain the illusion of authority and authenticity of their own power. Science and religion have long held a position of supremacy in the realms of morality and the truth, and neither will relinquish it or acknowledge a higher or more enlightened power without a fight, no matter how spiritual it may be. We are fortunate that a new breed of science is ready to challenge the establishment in a way that the general public would find impossible to do. This coupled with a change in peoples belief in the God given authority of the church, and the right of science and politicians to decide what we must believe in, is leading to a 'new age' of openness and the questioning of established 'truths'.

Education challenges reality; it's about empowering the learner to ask questions, to challenge the new as well as the old in order to seek out truth, no matter where it's hidden or how strange or uncomfortable it may first appear. If our beliefs and experiences challenge the established 'wisdom' of the day then as educators we must be prepared to examine vigorously all aspects of our knowledge in order to discover our objective truth in what we teach and believe. If Reiki is not what we think it is then we must have the courage and the desire to find out its true nature and the creative source we define as a wonderful Reiki experience. Personal development requires us to change and grow. Part of that growth means we will have to sooner or later, let go of things that that are proven no longer to be true, or beliefs that no longer support who we have become. Albert Einstein questioned the validity of his own scientific achievements when he said ''Now you think I am looking at my life's work with calm satisfaction. But there is not a single concept of which I am convinced that it will stand firm I am not sure if I was on the right track after all''.

As an individual I am sure of my own experiences, but as a teacher I must be sure to the best of my ability, knowledge and understanding the authenticity and validity of what I teach. I must be willing be to hold up my beliefs and experiences to the cold light of critical enquiry, to analyse and evaluate and not just perpetuate myths and legends in search of my objective truth.

A still quiet voice

In the darkness a still quiet voice spoke. It asked for mercy and compassion but no one listened. Softly, it asked for truth and justice but no one cared. Unheard but unbowed it would not be denied. As it grew in strength people began to listen, and in doing so the darkness of ignorance and fear began to fade.

With the light came understanding; mercy and compassion grew in the hearts of all men, and truth secured justice and freedom for all. With time mankind forgot these truths and the darkness returned. Slowly the voice of truth fell silent; mercy and compassion died in hearts that had grown cold with fear.

In our darkness a still quiet voice asks us to show mercy and compassion but will we listen? It asks each one of us to speak out for truth for justice but do we care? To hear we must listen with our hearts for its here that we find mercy and compassion. Truth and justice for all regardless of colour creed or religion, but only if there is enough light for us to see.

Chapter Twenty-Six

————◆◆◆————

Mastery is the acceptance of what we are not

————◆◆◆————

I don't refer to myself as a Reiki Master even though I have completed the necessary training and gained the certification allowing me to do so. But it's ok to be different isn't it? Different isn't just ok, it's vital for our development and growth as individuals and society as a whole. So to those who want to refer to themselves as a Reiki Master that's your prerogative, and I will always support your right to do so. In effect what I'm doing is exercising my right not to use that particular title, and give my reasons why I feel the title of Reiki teacher is far more appropriate to the work I do. If we look at a definition of Mastery we will see that it can be described as the 'possession or display of great skill, technique or knowledge that makes one master of a subject'. There's the rub; Reiki by our own definition is an expression of universal life energy, so can we in all honesty say that we have mastery over the infinite, I think not.

The problem we face is what we consider to be Reiki in the form of training manuals, hand positions, symbols and techniques isn't Reiki at all. They are simply a man made form of expression, a form of communication describing ways in which we may access and use the energetic power of Reiki. Esoteric teachings tell us that "the way that can be named is not the way" and using the same analogy we could say "the Reiki that can be written about is not Reiki". The study and production of Reiki training manuals and books like this one only allows us to lay claim to a certain level of academic knowledge and articulation. Reiki energy is just that; infinite energy in both name and nature.

There are those who say the title of Master is merely tradition and in some ways an honorary title but if we study both the eastern and westernised versions of Reiki story we find Dr Usui didn't use the title or refer to himself as a Master of Reiki or anything else. If we say we are following tradition, then we owe it to ourselves to ask whose traditions are we following and why. This title along with other changes such as the use of symbols, hand positions, rituals and in some cases the introduction of excessive training fees appears to be later additions to the Reiki time line. Dr Usui demonstrated Reiki and taught people plain and simple. It or he wasn't as far as I'm aware, prefixed with any creative title, these are just further examples of contemporary re-branding. Often when reading various training manuals you discover there are striking similarities in both content and layout, and in some cases are identical with only the front cover and branding showing any kind of creative individuality. If we wish to hold up the title of Reiki Master as some form of bench mark to personal commitment and achievement, we need to ensure our credibility isn't undermined by services and product quality that falls far below levels implied by grandiose titles. When you come down to it you do your research, you consider your options, make your choice and pay your money, in doing so you become part of the Reiki story.

People come to Reiki for varied and diverse reasons; some learn it but never use it, while others use it but have no desire to progress beyond the initial stages of their training. Of those who have the desire and ambition to progress through the advanced levels of training only a small proportion become teachers and that's ok.

Being different is more than just ok, it's vital to our personal development, health and wellbeing, for knowledge and understanding of oneself is the first part of the healing process.

It's also the first step on the road to recovery. Knowledge and understanding never comes to us complete; this is why we teach what we ourselves need to learn. By helping the student to find their path we as teachers are able to move closer to the truth that experience has shown lies before us as it unfolds one faltering step at a time. If you need to call yourself a master, go with it, but ask yourself why, only you can provide the answer. I am a Reiki teacher and practitioner first and foremost. The title of Master is one piece of baggage I have no desire to own. I have gained qualifications and experience in mainstream education specialising in challenging behaviour and complex educational needs to give both depth and breadth to my teaching of Reiki personal development, but I am still a work in progress.

Reiki is a wonderful thing; many things to many people, but one thing it's not is rocket science. It's inappropriate and misleading to make it out to be more complex than it is, and infer superiority by association or titles. As for me there may come a time in my spiritual and personal development when the title of Master may be appropriate but based on my progress so far, it certainly won't be in this life. When my time comes to return to my spiritual home and review my progress I'm sure I will see on my report card in red ink *'has potential but really must try harder'*. I will be ok with that, because it shows I'm heading in the right direction and one day I may just get there, wherever there may be.

We are children of the Universe

We are children of the Universe; our planet sustains us and the solar winds gift us the breath of life. Spirit is our true reflection mirroring our existence as we try to make sense of the images we see before us. In creation we see our beliefs reflected back to us.

Journey of illusion like Alice through the looking glass; an adventure fraught with danger and uncertainty, in truth there is no journey to be made. The key to our future lies within, hidden in clear sight so only the most determined seeker of truth may find it.

Life comes in many forms; there are many dimensions to knowledge and understanding, spirit is but one that awaits our awakening. We are not asked to be anything but ourselves; this growing awareness is truth demonstrated providing clarity to see we are closer than we think.

Knowledge and understanding never come to us complete; and the lessons we struggle to teach are the lessons we must first learn if we are to graduate from this school of life. Perfection is not required as it is incompatible with the spirit of free will. We are not asked to be perfect, mealy to attend and be present in the learning process of life.

Chapter Twenty-Seven

I can't unravel it, until I find the end

Development begins where the established ends; but the development of the new is not necessarily at the expense of the old. It's about building on what's gone before not automatically replacing it, for the purpose of all living things is to change, develop and grow. The established provides the foundation on which we build our new reality. It's part of human nature to try and improve on what's gone before, to adapt and overcome barriers and to go beyond the limitations placed upon us by tradition superstition, ignorance and fear. If this were not the case we would still be living in the dark ages. New ideas are challenged and often rejected, before eventually being considered and accepted. No matter how sound a new idea may be, if it challenges what is held to be true it also challenges the credibility of those who support those beliefs. When faced with the threat of new ideas, safety is found in numbers and defence of the old at the expense of the new often through ridicule and disinformation. We fear the unknown and what we don't understand, if it poses a big enough challenge to our established beliefs we will try to discredit, disregard or even destroy the threat no matter how worthy or spiritual it may be. Challenge the established belief and you challenge the values of the person who holds those beliefs, and in doing so undermine the foundations of everything they value and hold to be true.

Being right doesn't negate our responsibility to act with care and consideration for others or being aware of the consequences of our actions. Failing to do so we can fall prey to a 'right is might' mind set which is at odds with the concept of personal development. We can look to others to guide us but sooner or later we must break new ground and old truths in equal measure in order to find our own way in life. We are all different and one path is no better than another for they all eventually lead to knowledge and understanding of oneself.

Our uniqueness mean's that while we may share a similar experience what we take from that experience, the value we place upon it, and the lessons we choose to learn are subjective and meaningful to the individual. As such our role is not a passive one; it's an active participation which continually contributes to our personal, spiritual and social development.

One of the greatest barriers to this development is to place others on pedestals, then judge ourselves accordingly in relation to their lofty position of importance. To mistakenly believe their contribution is automatically more important or relevant than our own because of who they are. It does them a great disservice, and restricts our development by devaluing any contribution we make for ourselves. It's our life and we have a duty of care and responsibility to live it. To think we are not good enough is a limitation born out of ignorance and fear. This negative mindset restricts our development and stops us from becoming all that we can be. It's the mistakes we make, the lessons learnt and the life experiences gained that provides us with the necessary skills and abilities to grow and be all that we can be. Personal, spiritual and social development is only possible when we recognise and accept how little we know. It begins when we have the desire and courage to go beyond the barriers real or imaginary that restricts our progress. Stepping into the unknown where the established and accepted ends.

In choosing faith

In choosing faith before knowledge and understanding we create judgement and limitation. We measure self-worth by the choices we make and in doing so we alienate ourselves from those who we believe to be different.

The moment we become rigid in a belief we reject all others and our faith hardens with our resolve. The moment we say there is only one way those on a different path become lost souls requiring our salvation or enemies deserving of our mistrust.

The moment we believe that religion guarantees enlightenment we move further from the truth and damn those who do not share our beliefs. Faith alone is rigid in its application; it provides structure to our beliefs and a platform from which to stand in judgement on others.

Better to let go of faith in a single religion and recognise the truth shared by all spiritual teachings. Acknowledging perceived differences are no more than man's interpretation of a spiritual truth which asks us to seek out knowledge and understanding in all things.

Chapter Twenty-Eight

Changing the world is easy, changing me is the hard part

Progress is a process that never is complete. It's said if you give a man a fish, he will eat for a day, but if you teach him to fish he will eat for a lifetime. If we were to give the same man a new idea, he may consider it, but if we teach him to think he will discover within himself the power to change his world. Knowledge and understanding never comes complete; and it has to be said neither does personal development. A journey like any other; a journey of progress and delays, a journey of detours and dead ends, moments of elation when we can see so clearly; and dark days when we feel lost and overwhelmed by despair. On my own journey of discovery companions have been many, and each one has contributed to my personal development, their words of wisdom and encouragement have helped guide my faltering steps ever forward. Some challenged the beliefs I held about myself and dared me to come to the edge of uncertainty and fly. My writing has provided a freedom of expression and enabled me to become the narrator to my own life story, when pain and suffering silenced the child within, who even now so many years later still seeks to be heard. Part of this evolutionary process provides a milestone to help me gain perspective and direction. It also helps me to look back free from the emotional baggage carried for so long, to see just how far I have come. In helping others to help themselves we discover there is a fine line between education and indoctrination.

One encourages freedom of thought and the other enforces compliance. Indoctrination is thought reform; instilling ideas, attitudes, and beliefs often by coercion or subversion. The indoctrinated person is expected to get with the programme, accepting without question what they have learned. Analytical abilities in the individual are suppressed and the focus is on following the social heard. By comparison education is a process of personal growth by means of study and learning, developing the mind to gain knowledge and understanding. Education isn't about telling the person what to think, but empowering them to think objectively for themselves and where necessary challenge what they hold to be true. Education asks us to loosen our grip on reality and embrace the new and unknown, but sometimes before we can we have to unpick the restrictions indoctrination uses to manipulate and control our thoughts, beliefs and actions

Unfortunately, sometimes the conditioning runs so deep, is so well established when presented with a new idea or belief, some find it almost impossible to accept causing mental and emotional distress. This condition is called cognitive dissonance and occurs when a person is faced with two or more deep seated contradictory beliefs. This is why if we don't believe at a deep and meaningful level, the changes we are being asked to accept we will revert back to the old way of thinking and established patterns at the first opportunity. We are creatures of habit and routine and internal consistency is comforting. Conflicting ideal makes us feel uncomfortable and we will do anything to reduce that conflict, or reject the cause of the discomfort, anything that could cause us to change what we hold to be true.

A story called 'Life'

What we prize and hold dear is set by the value of our beliefs. Our attitude to life and the challenges we face is nurtured by our beliefs, the choices we make are then influenced by what we believe to be true.

Self-image and self-worth developed at an early age is forged by the beliefs and values of others. We attempt only what

we think possible and only what we believe we deserve to achieve. Those thoughts and beliefs construct our path, the direction we take, and our ultimate destination.

Reality is the fabric of life; woven by experiences we have created. Framed by our thoughts and beliefs it provides a canvas upon which our life is recorded. A testament of what was, what is, and what can be.

Change is inevitable; development only becomes an option when we recognise and accept we have the power to break new ground and old truths in equal measure.

Beliefs are the stuff of myths and legend and we are both author and narrator of our story called life.

Chapter Twenty-Nine

The stranger that lives my life

Most people don't know who they really are, and some go through their whole lives without taking the time to get to know the stranger that lives their life. Sometimes it takes a traumatic event or a life changing wake up call to get us to stop and re-evaluate our lives. To look at what's important, and ask ourselves why we believe what we do. We come into this world unbiased, uncluttered, and free from any preconceived ideas about ourselves or those around us. To use a contemporary analogy we enter the world a pristine system ready to accept all of the down loads that's available; unfortunately, we don't have a virus protection so we pick up everything that's going. The vast majority of our beliefs, values, fears, and ideas have been given to us by others, and we accepted them as our own simply because we knew no better. Those around us automatically become our teachers whether they are qualified or suitable for the task. During our formative years everyone we come in contact with becomes an influential force in our lives. The closer the relationship the stronger the bond, and the greater the influence and control they have over us. The problem is teachers can only teach us what they themselves have learnt, and although we eventually create our own experiences these are still influenced by what we believe and the way we have learned to think.

Many experts believe that by the age of three we have a clear sense of identity of who we are, and how we fit in with those around us. In this sense our knowledge and understanding is more traditional and conditional, than educational. It's only when we take time to evaluate our beliefs and thought processes can we begin to gain some understanding of who we are, and what this growing personal awareness means to us. It's about discovering the truth about who we are; who and what contributed to making us the way we are, and its only when we begin to understand ourselves can we be sure which of our beliefs, values, and fears we can truly call our own.

This process can be very liberating, as we reclaim our personal power through the letting go of other people's stuff, and stop taking responsibility for other people's actions. It's also very empowering as we ask the question; is what I believe about myself supporting my idea of who I am, and what I want to be? Liberating to budding free thinkers who want to understand themselves, but very frightening to those who don't like change and would rather things stay the way they are no matter how bad they appear to be. Hanging onto what they perceive as their stuff, illness is an excellent example of what people claim ownership for, it gives some a sense of identity and purpose in life. They identify with their condition and some would rather die than change the way they think and believe about themselves.

We should never assume what we think is the norm. Just because we think it and know it in our own mind doesn't automatically make it so. Others may not share our views or think the same way we do. From their perspective or point of view, they are right and it's we who are wrong. In one sense they are right. We can all be blind to the obvious and to a certain extent this is created by the way our brain works in its effort to make sense of the world we live in, and what we hold to be true.

The Circle of Stones

From afar I see its cold grey fingers break the skyline as if reaching to the heavens in praise of the old ways that gave them life. Silhouetted against the morning sky they are a testament of a belief long past, and the faith of those who placed them there. I

205

*stare in wonder at the circle of stones that stands before me;
hard and unyielding like guardians emerging out of the morning
mists ready to challenge my presence here.*

*As I enter the circle of stones I find a place of solitude
within. Sunlight bathes the ground and the warm air is cut by the
cool dark shadows of this ancient monument. As if embraced the
energy of my ancestors welcomes me home as I search for
knowledge and understanding of our spiritual traditions.*

*In the silence the only sounds are those of my beating
heart and my thoughts which seem to echo within this place of
peace and contemplation. Making a pilgrimage of discovery I
return to a place of learning and in doing so I take my rightful
place among those who have gone before, and I become part of
the story of the stones.*

*Within the circle I feel the quickening as spirit moves
within me as if the earth beneath my feet, the mountains, and the
sky above are acknowledging the offerings of thanks I bring to
lay before them.*

*A sanctuary to still the mind and an oasis to refresh the
spirit; in silence I bow my head and give thanks for all that I
have received, and in doing so my journey ends within the
stones, and the circle is complete.*

Chapter Thirty

The far side of my fear

Fear like any emotion becomes an experience the moment we become aware of it, and like any story, there are always two sides to every emotion and every experience. Until we personally experienced something it remains no more than an intellectual concept, it's only when we become aware of it and experience it first-hand does it become 'real' and we make it our own. In the same way we can pick up a book and read the story of Reiki and the Usui legend, it's only when we come to Reiki and embrace both the spirit and the letter can it become a 'real' life changing experience. We can sympathise and empathise with another's predicament but until we have experienced a similar circumstance ourselves we have no real understanding of how that person may be feeling or what they have gone through. Only when we speak from a place of personal experience can the words "I know what you are going through" begin to take on real value and meaning.

Even then, emotions and feelings are subjective and unique to the person experiencing them. How one person reacts or responds to a particular situation can be totally different to another faced with the same set of circumstances. Life is full of examples of people overcoming life threatening challenges whilst others seemed unable to effectively deal the everyday obstacles that life places before them.

Fear by definition is focused on the future; in much the same way that regret is rooted in the past. Yet both have the power to debilitate us in the here and now. Fear is a feeling of apprehension and foreboding, a dread of some event that has not happened. As such, no matter how real the fear may feel, it is only our personal interpretation of 'one possible outcome' that owes more to the quality of our mindset and thought processes, than certainty of the future. To fully understand and control our fears we must first be aware of them and experience them to the point we can exorcise them. If we try to run from our fears we simply strengthen their existence. Fear is a parasite fed by ignorance and resistance, and what we resist will most definitely persist. We must be able to work through our fear, to understand it, and then disempower it through knowledge, and understanding of its true nature.

The only person we can truly heal is ourselves; and the healing of oneself only becomes possible through the raising of our knowledge and understanding. Fear is like an elusive shadow; we feel its effects without being able to physically get hold of it, and unless we understand the nature of fear we will always feel powerless to overcome it. This is why the physical reality is always easier to deal with. How many times have we heard the words, or even said it ourselves as we emerge from the far side of a fearful situation "it' wasn't as bad as I thought it would be". This is because fear not only fills us with dread it also undermines our confidence and gets us to doubt ourselves and our ability to deal with life effectively.

You have survived countless stressful situations where you had little or no experience and your fear of the unknown made you question whether you would be able to get through the challenges ahead. We are survivors born of survivors and no matter how weak or afraid we may feel in the midst of fear, we are far stronger than we can ever imagine. Once we have found the strength to work through our fears and experience them from both sides the process will become easier as knowledge and understanding allows us to regain control over our thoughts, feelings and emotions. Nature has gifted us a built in fight of flight response and our natural reaction is to run from anything that frightens us, be it real or imaginary. Unfortunately our brain can't differentiate between a real danger and an emotionally charged fearful mental image of a perceived threat. Both have the power to create an adverse effect on our physical, emotional and psychological wellbeing by flooding our system with stress hormones. This fight or flight response is appropriate when there is a real and present danger, but we must learn to distinguish between the perception and the reality. If we are not careful the old acronym of a fear; 'False Expectation Appearing Real' can immobilise us as we can become paralysed by our own thoughts, and become jailors to our own mental and emotional confinement.

Experience may not provide us with a 'get out of jail free card' but it will provide us with the key to understanding the true nature of our fears and the illusionary power they hold over us. Unfortunately that key is to be found on the far side of our fears.

Chapter Thirty-One

Ok you can fix me, but leave my life alone

When we think of healing we automatically think of healing the physical body, illnesses and diseases needing to heal and a body to be made well. But we are more than a physical body and we can never be totally separated from life around us. If healing of the body, the physical ailment is our priority we can become distracted by the symptoms and miss the underlying causes of the conditions. The link between our mind and our body is well documented if not necessarily understood. Our psychology becomes our biology; which means our thoughts have the power and the ability to directly affect our body and influence the way in which it works. We are not just talking about our emotions or mental capacity; our thoughts connect to the very core of our being, the way in which our DNA works and the effect this has on every cell in our body.

Our thoughts are more vibrational than they are pictorial and it's their vibrational content that holds the power to influence change, to heal or impede health and wellbeing. The vibrational frequency of our thoughts can either resonate in a life affirming way, or create discord within us, put simply, they have the power to make us well, or to make us ill, and we have a duty of care to decide which it should be.

The inner is the mirror upon which the outer is reflected; the inner is the cause and the outer is the effect and as the vibration of our thoughts affects us at a cellular level they also have the power to influence the energy that surrounds us. Our thoughts can be defused to the point where they create a gentle ripple effect upon the surrounding energy field, or they can be focussed and directed in the form of our attention and intention. Our attention is what we focus on, and our intention is what we choose to do about it. If the quality of our thoughts, their frequency has the power to affect the world around us then we must face up to the fact that we have a personal and collective responsibility for the quality of our thoughts and the world they are helping to create socially, nationally and globally. The idea that we are separated by distance is as illusionary as the belief that we are defined and segregated by colour, creed or religion. The idea of separation must first establish a place in the mind before it can seek expression in life, correct the thought and you change the nature of the experience that must come from it. To say we live in the universe denotes a sense of separation from the world around us and can reinforce a feeling of isolation. When we change our perception and view ourselves not as separate entities but as unique yet indivisible expressions of the universe itself, we can't help but see we are one with creation in all of its many forms.

By nature of our thought processes we segregate and compartmentalise aspects of our lives and if we are not careful we can adopt the same limiting approach to the healing that may need to take place. Healing is never about separation; to heal is to make whole, to bring together and unify through the acquisition and application of knowledge and understanding is a prerequisite for healing of any description to take place. If we wish to heal ourselves we must begin with our thoughts, the beliefs they help create, and the actions we then take based on what we then hold to be true. This framework is the life we have created, but to heal we must begin to think outside of the box. We are the one constant, the one common denominator of every experience we have ever created and lived through. Your mind can be viewed as the creative centre of our personal microscopic universe and you are the sole creator of those thoughts and through that creative process you have fabricated every aspect of your life. Areas, which may or may not, require our attention. Situations, circumstances or relationships that need to be addressed and healed but are missed, overlooked or simply ignored because we have become distracted, sometimes willingly, by a high profile physical condition that has grabbed our attention.

Healing that only deal with the obvious symptoms is nothing more than first aid that does little to address the underlying issues, and as such the root cause remains established and untouched waiting to re-establish itself at the first opportunity. Roots buried deep; out of sight yet with the potential to connect and affect seemingly unrelated aspects of our lives. The healing of one wound may take us on a journey to discover a hurt buried so deep that has without us realising it, affected every part of our life, and touched every relationship we have had in life.

To heal ourselves we must be willing and able to first look within to find, recognise and accept the causal effect of our thoughts, beliefs and actions on the life we have created for ourselves, and our relationship with those around us. Then, we must turn our attention to the various aspects of our lives we have compartmentalised; open the boxes to see what action if any needs to be taken in order for healing to take place and so integrate it with the healing of the whole person, the whole life. A life brought into balance; a life not of unrealistic perfection but one of grounded reality that can accept and embrace both beauty and imperfection without harsh and unnecessary judgement. A life that recognises that the past present and future are inexorably connected and in healing the past we release the present from the pain and suffering and create a healthy and life affirming future. Healing is not complete until it has been assimilated in mind, body and spirit. We are not complete until we are able to assimilate all of the different parts of our life in order to make whole and heal ourselves. To heal is to educate and through knowledge and understanding we come to recognise that healing of self can never be separated from life because we are one and the same.

Chapter Thirty-Two

Making us whole again

When we seek to become whole we must not only recognise and accept our dark side, we must acknowledge it as a great teacher and the wisdom it brings. We are spiritual beings evolving through a physical experience, and as such we are composed of both light and darkness. Our spiritual essence is the light; mortality provides the shadow and is home to our ignorance and darkest fears. When we take our first faltering steps on our pilgrimage to become whole, we mistakenly believe this requires a change of identity, to get rid of anything in our personality and character that isn't good or wholesome. Some go to great lengths to get rid of elements of their personality they don't like, believing they are in some way damaged and imperfect. If we take a moment to step back from this conflict and consider what it actually means to make whole we begin to get a completely different perspective on the challenge before us. By definition to be whole means amongst other things, to be complete undivided and intact. To be in one piece, sound unbroken or unimpaired with no part removed. A thing that is healthy and complete in itself. All of which appears to be in direct opposition to the physical, mental and emotional anguish we put ourselves through in order to fit this spiritual stereotype. Obviously the concept and reality are at odds and if we are not careful we can become a casualty caught between these opposing factions.

The Yin and Yang colour co-ordination is not accidental; it demonstrates clearly that the concept of being whole is not monochrome. To be whole requires us to acknowledge the character and strength that both darkness and light bring to the union and the perspective it gifts us. Mother Nature is a great teacher; if we have the good sense to listen and observe we can learn so much. Her progress and development are both transitional and seasonal, encompassing both light and dark and a multitude of shades in between.

She does not favour one season above the other for she knows that without the cold and darkness of winter there would be no summer to celebrate and enjoy.

We are creatures of habit and imperfection by default. It's through those imperfections we are gifted the opportunity to grow, for perfection is incompatible with change and development. It's not about wallowing in the darkness of our imperfections or basking in the glow of some perceived spiritual ideal, it's about embracing all of the different facets that go to make up who we are. Most importantly it's about recognising the potential to be all that we can be, potential that can only be realised through raised awareness, knowledge and understanding of our true self, and the complete unification of the mind, body and spirit. There is nothing new to be found in our comfort zone and growth is only possible when we have the courage to venture beyond what we already know and the limitations we have set ourselves. Strength is born out of weakness and courage develops not through the absence of fear but through adversity faced and overcome no matter how afraid we may be. To be whole we need to shift our focus away from imperfections real or imaginary, which in reality provide us with the raw materials to all constructive development. The only darkness we need to rid ourselves of is the darkness of ignorance and fear that both blinds and binds us.

Healing of any kind is only made possible through the acquisition and application of knowledge and understanding. This is the light of awareness that seeks not to segregate or destroy but to bring together, unify and make whole that which we fear is broken.

Chapter Thirty-Three

Blame always hides behind a belief

Human nature being what it is, the minute something goes wrong in our life we look for someone to blame. We either blame someone else regardless of whether it's their fault or not, if we suffer from low self-esteem we mistakenly believe that this problem like all others is automatically our fault. Even when caught making a simple mistake or doing something wrong, we will often go to great lengths to justify our actions and defend ourselves. Even to the point of blaming the other person for our actions, it's almost like we had a right to do what we did because of the other person or the situation. The root cause of all of our conscious actions is a creative belief that formulates our lives and everything in it. We do what we do because it serves a purpose no matter how negative or self-destructive our actions may appear. The police say that "to understand a crime you need to understand the motive", for us to understand our own behaviour or anyone else we need to understand the creative belief that determines who we are, and why we do what we do. Mistakes can be seen as a natural part of our personal growth and development, and not indicative of being in any way a bad person.

Blame can seem like a natural and justified reaction, but blame for its own sake can lead us into a dead end of resentment and recrimination. Accepting responsibility for our actions is a creative response that can lead to development and growth, but true responsibility only comes with knowledge and understanding.

Once we begin to understand why we think and act in a way we do, we can direct our intention towards change rather than repetition, positive response rather than a negative reaction. Attention and intention is our belief in action; it is the power of positive change, we do only what we believe is possible, and the quality of our intention determines the quality of our actions and attitude we present to others.

Every challenge will trigger a response in some form or another, when we apportion blame we are challenging a belief and indirectly the person that holds that belief. Every action we take brings with it a set of consequences that must then be dealt with in order to move forward. We are motivated, directed, and defined by our self-belief, our relationship to the world we live in and the people around us. Understand the nature of the belief and you will begin to understand the person that holds those beliefs and the life they lead. From this we can see that knowing oneself is the beginning of true knowledge and understanding and the end of the need to blame ourselves, or anyone else.

Chapter Thirty-Four

Knowledge and understanding

are the physicians of mind, body and soul

The duty of a teacher is to educate; to illuminate the path of learning and elucidate a mind where ignorance and fear prevails. This we do this, not by telling the student what to think, but by challenging what they already hold to be true. Our role is to guide and help them break free of ignorance and fear formed by conditioning, tradition and dogma. We dare them to consider new thoughts and ideas that have the power to change their perception of reality and in doing so they can begin to take responsibility for their own learning. It is said that 'we teach what we wish to learn' and in many ways this is true, for knowledge and understanding never comes to us complete, and on our journey of exploration to find the truth, knowledge and understanding helps illuminate the path that opens up before us as the teacher and student walk side by side. A teacher never seeks to condition or control; they seek to empower by helping the student to free their spirit, and their mind. Their questions should never be seen as a challenge to authority but as an expression of their desire to learn and understand.

The dark ages were unable to hold captive those who had the courage to question what was then held to be true, and overcome the barriers to development, real or imaginary. Education is a physician of the mind and the body, for without the attendance of knowledge and understanding the healing of the patient, and the freeing of the mind is impossible. Symptoms of ignorance and fear may be addressed on a superficial level, but the root cause will go untouched. A closed mind is unaware of its own ignorance and the self imposed limitations that restrict its development and growth. Changed against its will, it remains connected to its roots and will at the first opportunity seek to return to the comfort of the beliefs and values it holds to be true. Education is the only viable means of introducing and maintaining sustainable change in the individual and in society as a whole. Reward and punishment are limited in their concept and application, for as with any addiction their use and application will have to be increased in order to maintain a level of control. Empower a person to take responsibility to think for themselves and you help free them from the control of conditioning, tradition and dogma and the many prejudices they help perpetuate. Every person has a personal best and it's the role of the teacher and mentor to help them achieve it whatever it may be.

Everyone has the capacity to learn but some may not be ready and willing to do so, as teachers we help those that we can and gently sow the seeds of learning that one day may come to fruition in another time, another place, with teacher better suited to the needs of the developing student. Like ripples spreading out beyond our horizon to rest upon far distant shores, knowledge and understanding has the power to transcend time and affect in a positive and life affirming way of generations to come.

Chapter Thirty-Five

Your words changed my life. No, they haven't ....

you did

We appear to be drawn to short cuts and easy options, with quick fixes the order of the day. Instant results and instant gratification are usually short lived leaving us searching for the next fix to make us feel good about ourselves. We often read about certain spiritual words or meaningful phrases powerful enough to change your life, and all you have to do is read them for the magic to happen. A nice comforting thought, but life doesn't work like that. As long as we buy into the belief that others have the power to change our life for us we are locked into a victim mentality. Unfortunately, words in themselves don't have the power to change your life. Life changes; circumstances may change, but ultimately people change as a consequence of taking action. Words are signposts that can help redirect our thoughts, hopefully resonating with us in such a way that they stimulate a re-evaluation of what we hold to be true and the way we live our lives. Stripped back and basic the process becomes very simple to implement and understand. If you want different, do different and change is guaranteed.

It can be evolutionary or revolutionary; but change of any description requires a catalyst to trigger the process. Inspirational words can act as a catalyst but they require two other components for change to become a reality. If words act as a signpost, then hopefully they will help us find within ourselves the desire for change and a willingness to take action. The value of signposts lies in their ability to give direction, but no matter how informative they may be they can't make the journey for us. We alone have the power to take the steps necessary to change the direction life takes.

Chapter Thirty-Six

Loosen your grip on reality, what is, and what can be

When it comes to learning we are all different. There are seven recognised modalities of learning and these are visual, aural, verbal, physical, logical, social and finally solitary. We learn in different ways, and the way we process and retain new information. Whether we realise it or not, we all have blind spots when it comes to changing our beliefs and the way we think, which is exactly how we are supposed to accept new knowledge and understanding in the first place. We share learning preferences, learning differences and more importantly favourite beliefs about ourselves we want to hang on to. Learning is a process of change and development; it's about loosening our grip on the reality we have come to believe in, and the reality of what can be, embracing uncertainty and the unknown. People are comfortable with accepting new ideas as long as they don't challenge the old ways.

When it does we try to use the new to validate or justify the old way of doing things, if the new appears too extreme or challenging we will reject it out of hand or revert back to the comfort of the tried and tested at the first opportunity. Unfortunately, we can't develop and grow and stay where we are at the same time. Change and uncertainty are the basis of the learning experience, while certainty requires a sense of permanency and is opposed to progress and development. Knowledge and understanding never comes to us complete so the learning it brings is transitional; and this state of change is the only real constant in life. No matter how stable or fixed a thing may first appear it is in a constant process of transformation. Nature is the ultimate teacher and shows us nothing stays the same indefinitely. Our resistance comes primarily from a need to feel in control and from a fear of losing something that we have claimed ownership to, no matter how unhelpful or unhealthy it may be. In resisting we fight to stay where we are and hang on to what makes us feel safe and secure, even if it's no longer valid or outgrown. A great deal of unnecessary stress anxiety and tension are caused by our unwillingness to accept what is. Reality is positional; it gives us a point of reference and a direction which is necessary to bring about the change we desire. This is where I am, this is where I want to be, this is the route that will get me there.

We fear and distrust anything or anyone who appears different to our rigid definition of normal, different is change by another name, and we fear and distrust what we don't understand be it a person, belief or a new way of thinking. Yet belief is often nothing more than make-believe, a feeling of certainty; we are certain of what we believe and those beliefs provide us with the evidence and proof of our convictions. If we aren't careful we can box ourselves in by a rigid and closed mindset. A 'box' we must then learn to dismantle or think outside of, if we wish to find innovation and motivation for personal development.

Few if any of our beliefs are new or original, they are hand me downs passed from generation to generation, usually by our parents, peer groups and adults in a position of influence. In effect they all took on the role of teacher and we were the blank page upon which 'our' beliefs were laid down. With a child's innocence and knowing no better we accepted them as our own. We should never blame ourselves or our teachers for those truths we can no longer accept without question, for they could only teach us what they themselves learnt. But acceptance of the new should never automatically be at the expense of the old; both the new and the tried and tested should be challenged and held to the light of scrutiny, to establish their truth, validity and worth.

Life is a process of constant change; it can be evolutionary learning from past mistakes, where the new is an extension of the old, and builds on the foundations laid by what has gone before. Or it can be revolutionary in its desire to sweep away the old and replace it with a new set of values and beliefs. In reality there is nothing new under the sun and what goes around will eventually come around again? The present moment is an extension of what was, and will be again, albeit in a different format. It may look different and have a different title but even the new owes its existence to the knowledge and understanding that made it possible.

The understanding of one self and recognising the belief based limitations we hold onto, and those we see as different, is the first step in being able to understand and appreciate the value of others. A name is just a label that we attach to those who look different, behave differently, and have a different faith or culture. The moment we label certain groups or individuals in a less than empowering way we define ourselves more than we do them.

Learning requires us to look beyond the superficial labels that separate and find the common ground we share. We must be able to acknowledge and respect the person beneath labels we have placed on them, the baggage they carry, and the belief based limitations they have to deal with. Judgement is a luxury we can't afford. A single step to one person may be a milestone to another; all achievement is relevant to the progress we are able to make, and the personal barriers we have the strength and courage to overcome. We all have learning difficulties to one degree or another; we have belief based limitations and favourite ideas that keep us locked in our comfort zone. When we come down to it, we are all blind when it comes to seeing things we don't want to face up to and deal with. It's not about judging ourselves or others harshly for some perceived weakness or deficiency, it's about understanding and developing a willingness to loosen our grip on reality, letting go of old ideas and beliefs that no longer support us, reflect the person we have become or more importantly the person we aspire to become.

Chapter Thirty-Seven

Experience will always seek to find expression

Experience seeks expression. Writing provides a means of communication where, as the author, we can become the narrator of our life story. When unable to speak the words, writing allows the pain of the past to gain recognition and bring about the closure necessary for the present moment to take its rightful place in our life. In telling the story we can gain clarity, and when we can recount our story without the shedding of tears we know the healing of that particular chapter in life is complete.

Writing is a process of self-discovery during which we can bring closure to the past while creating a future we wish to experience. Knowledge and understanding of oneself is the true healer and when we can make peace with our past we are free to part on good terms.

Chapter Thirty-Eight

A short cut to Assumption

No matter how unsound the practice is we are all guilty of making assumptions in life. If we take a moment to consider it, it's almost second nature as we do it without thinking, which in effect, is what making assumptions is all about. A judgement call made without the thought processes necessary to give it value or meaning.

A short cut made up of assumptions, suppositions and a path of least resistance that leads us to take so much for granted.

A dangerous short cut that bypasses the need or desire to question, challenge or provide the proof necessary to validate what we hold to be true. Like invisible string joining up the dots of life. We judge because it's easier than thinking, assumption is the easiest form of judgment because it requires no thinking at all.

Chapter Thirty-Nine

A partnership for change

Whatever we do repeatedly we do so for a reason or a reward. The habits we develop and the experiences we create no matter how negative fulfil a deep seated need within us. This need is linked directly to a belief we hold about ourselves, if you change the belief you will ultimately change the habit and the corresponding experience it creates. When the need no longer exists, the habit or routine that feeds it is no longer required and becomes redundant. Raised awareness that comes with knowledge and understanding is the first step in any form of change, be it a direction in life or the healing of oneself. Every situation we experience is in the same moment a combination of the past, present and future rolled into one.

Action taken in the past created the present moment, and what we do now will create a future we must experience and live through. To know where you want to be you must first understand where you are and what brought you to this place in time. This provides a point of departure and a destination, a place or a state of mind. Knowing change is required is only the first step; knowing we have a problem is one thing but knowing what to do about it is another. This is where a partnership for change can begin to create a positive effect in our lives. Teachers and signposts have a lot in common; they don't tell you what you must do. Their role is to simply point the way and if necessary provide directions. All any teacher can hope to do is bring about that initial state of awareness by helping the student take responsibility for their own learning. A teacher's role is to show the way but never impose limitations by telling the student what they must see, or what they must think. Personal development is just that, each one has a responsibility and duty of care for our health and wellbeing because no one else can do it for us.

The decision always rests with us as to whether we make the changes necessary or we choose to stay the way we are bogged down by old habits and stale routines or worst still, immobilised by ignorance and fear. We must have the determination to make the changes necessary, knowing where you want to go and knowing how to get there is one, thing but planning and preparation in itself won't get the job done or achieve your goal. Sooner or later you have to set off taking the first faltering steps on your journey. A new and exciting adventure or a journey of self-discovery to get to know the person you have become, the principles are exactly the same.

Sooner or later you will have to let go of the past and commit your time and energy to a new course of action in order to achieve lasting and sustainable change in your life. Others can provide the knowledge and understanding and help point the way but you must have the desire, belief and determination to make it happen. A belief no matter how deep seated is no more than a feeling of certainty. We are certain of our beliefs and what we are able to achieve, and whatever we believe about ourselves becomes our truth, and it's those beliefs we hold about ourselves that helps form the world we create. We simply have to decide on the kind of world we wish to live in.

Chapter Forty

I may be spiritual, but am I for real?

When we look to define the word 'authentic' we come up with a number of definitions that can help us understand what an authentic person may look like. To be authentic you must not be a copy, false or an imitation. You will be real, you will be genuine in the way you represent your true nature or beliefs. You will be true to yourself and as such worthy of acceptance for who and what you are.

In spite of the artificial and sometimes illusionary barriers and borders created by politics and religion to keep us segregated for the purpose of manipulation and control, we co-exist on this planet with approximately eight billion other souls who share more similarities than they do differences. They may look like different makes and models, but we all came off the same production line and we all conform to the same genetic blueprint. But with so many people on this planet unless we are sure of our own personal identity it becomes easy to get lost in the crowd; to blend in becomes a greater attraction than the desire to stand out and be recognised as an individual in our own right. There is safety in numbers and security of a shared comfort zone that takes away the pressure of individual thought and action, allowing us to go with the flow, in the belief that we can't all be wrong.

Authenticity requires a reality check; authenticity can't be verified unless we have the courage and desire to strip away the years of conditioning placed upon us by parents and role models in our formative years, by tradition, social expectation and dogma. Each in their way covers us with a veneer of conformity that eventually hides the true personality within. If we desire to be authentic then the first step is to recognise and accept it's an inside job, an internal journey that we alone can make in order to meet and get to know this stranger that lives our life, and reach a point of self-realisation. It has to be said, this isn't for the faint hearted. As each layer is considered, to be retained or discarded, our personalised comfort zone shrinks until the only thing left to face is our true self. Self that is stripped back and devoid of pretence; no longer able to hide behind expedient beliefs and values.

To authenticate the true self takes both time and effort. In a society that values artificial reality and celebrity status above the truth, it's much easier to create the illusion of authenticity by adopting a wide range of in vogue personas. Off the peg values, beliefs and opinions that can be mixed and matched to suit all occasions. Disguises that become nothing more than another layer that hides the person within. Those who seek to hide their true nature from even their own reflection, live in fear of the day the mirror loses its power to lie and they see nothing but empty eyes and an empty life reflected back to them. Spirituality doesn't grant special dispensation to those who would look to hide their true personality in the trappings of Namaste, love and light or blessing be; nor does it own the monopoly on righteousness. The true nature of spirituality lies not in its name or what we perceive it to be. It's found in the smallest action expressed it in our daily lives. Some may seek to wear it as a mantle to cover and conceal, while others use the light they find within to uncover their own shadows in an effort to achieve transparency and their authenticity.

Chapter Forty-One

What we focus on; what it means,

and what we choose to do about it

This is the magic formula for creation, all manner of change, personal development and self-healing. What we focus on engages our attention; what it means to us helps define the nature of our attitude and the personal value we place upon it. What we choose to do about it engages and directs our intention towards a perceived outcome. Any formula, magic or otherwise must first be understood and then implemented consistently in order to achieve any kind of effective results. Focus and consistency are the keys to long term success, if we can't maintain our attention and intention on what we have set out to achieve we shouldn't be surprised when we fail to get the results we were hoping for. Intermittent commitment and effort will always be reflected negatively in an unsatisfactory outcome. Winners win consistently because of the unwavering belief and commitment in their ability to achieve their goal. When ability is on a par with others it's mental strength and superior attitude that separates the ultimate winner from the also ran.

This formula is powerful because it works, but unfortunately we don't always work in the way we should. Life is never static and has an annoying habit of getting in the way and distracting us from the task in hand. What appear to be more urgent priorities push in and grab our attention. Before we know where we are we have begun to lose ground as our goal drifts further and further away from us. We are human with frailties and failings and these can sometimes be the greatest barriers we have to overcome. We get disheartened and disillusioned when the perceived results aren't what we think they should be. We get distracted by life and we get lazy putting off what we know we should be doing, we promise to do twice as much tomorrow to make up for lost time. A promise made with the best of intentions, but a promise we very rarely if ever keep.

I call it a magic formula but there is no such thing. The surest way to experience the future you desire is to create it. This you can only do if your thoughts, belief and actions are in harmony with one another, if they lack resonance there will be discord, disruption and confusion. If you are prepared to leave your future to chance and the fickle hand of fate then you have no one to blame but yourself when your life doesn't appear to be working in the way you wanted, or hoped it would. It is often said life isn't fair; no its not, and it's not meant to be. This idea of fairness works on the principle of a benevolent universe that has in some way failed to do its job properly to protect nice people from nasty things happening. The reality is, the universe neither rewards nor punishes; it simply harmonises and responds to the energetic information it receives from us. Its currency is energy; its denominations are frequency and vibration, and it's our duty of care, our responsibility to understand the nature of the environment in which we choose to live our life. In the physical sense; as to the kind of life we have chosen to lead, and the life choices we make on a daily basis. On an energy level, our relationship with the universe and the way it's continuously responding to the energy of our thoughts, beliefs and actions.

We have a direct line and whether we realise it or not, what we focus on, what it means to us, and what we choose to do about it is communion with the universe. A universe that never disconnects us, a universe that is always listening and once we realise the true nature of our relationship, we begin to understand that no prayer goes unanswered.

Chapter Forty-Two

Taking action is your super power

Our lives change in an instant; the moment we take action. Change only takes as long as the action it takes to creates it. Our time is eaten up by procrastination, thinking about change, wondering and worrying about change, but change itself is instant. There is always something to know before there is something to do, but over thinking can immobilise us and stop us taking action. Thinking is necessary, consideration is a safeguard, but it should not become a substitute for making decisions and taking the action that bring about change in our lives. Any action is change in itself; the act of doing anything automatically changes the present moment and creates a different future with the potential for countless outcomes.

Thinking about change is a process of mental theorising, a decision is the catalyst, and our action creates the experiences. Ignorance, lacking knowledge and understanding, creates fear which stops us from changing and it's these fears that immobilise our ability to make decisions about our lives. We become conditioned to fear failure, believing it's better to procrastinate than to make a decision that could be wrong. We have convinced ourselves that inaction is far better than failure; if we act we run the risk of getting it wrong and it's better to be safe than sorry. Unfortunately we are controlled by our perception of reality and not by reality itself.

What we focus on we empower, its value is based on our beliefs, and it's those beliefs that determine whether we take a chance and change, or play it safe and stay where we are. We are motivated to do things we enjoy and give us pleasure which helps create a mental and emotional comfort zone. We are also motivated by our survival instinct to stay away from anything that causes us discomfort or pain. It's these neurological associations that determine whether we will link taking action to pleasure or to pain. If we see change as a pleasurable experience we will find taking action much easier than if we associate change or the decision making process with the discomfort associated with stepping outside of our comfort zone.

If sustained emotional responses become associated with the person, place, or experience that helped created that emotion, so just thinking about a certain situation can trigger the emotion, good or bad. Once we come to believe that the world is a dangerous place, love hurts, and people can't be trusted the associations are established. This creates our sphere of perception, and determines how we react to those situations from that point on.

These negative beliefs can stop us being happy and living life to the full, and if we are not careful we can become imprisoned by beliefs created by fear rather than an informed and meaningful experience. The good news is that awareness is nearly as powerful as action, and being aware of any situation is the first step in changing it. A change in how we view something provides us with options and new ways of dealing with old situations. All we have to do is start asking questions of ourselves. Why do we feel, think, and react the way we do in certain situations, are these reactions based on knowledge and understanding or are they fear driven, or misplaced emotions that no longer represent who we are.

Success and failure walk hand in hand and not every action will get us the results we desire, but those who are afraid to fail will also be afraid to step out of their comfort zone, take chances and try something new. It takes personal courage to change and we must be flexible in our approach to achieving what we want. We must be willing to adapt and overcome, adjust while staying focussed on our long term objectives, for it's the things that we do consistently that create long term results. Thinking is theoretical it allows us to conceptualise; to revisit what we already know and ponder the, what if's of life. It's the true power of action that releases potential and creates the experiences we desire. Action creates movement and direction; it's your actions, not your conditioning that has the power to create the life you want.

It's impossible to change and stay the way you were; development is life in action and all living things by their very nature must develop and grow. We have a choice and we must decide the way in which we live our life. We can remain in the darkness of ignorance and fear or we can grow towards the light of knowledge and understanding. We have the power to create that change; that power is our ability to take action, and the moment we do so, we will have begun to create the kind of future we want to experience.

Chapter Forty-Three

If I try I may fail;

that's ok, you are allowed

Imagine if you would a journey undertaken that must be successfully navigated in order to reach your destination, using the most up to date GPS technology available. Would your journey be made any easier by the presence of its mocking disembodied voice as it criticised you for the choices you made as you struggled to navigate the obstacles before you? Would it help if it berated you when you took a wrong turning, bringing you to a standstill as you faced a dead end?

Would you gain encouragement as it laughed at your fear and confusion when you didn't know which way to turn? Would you grow in confidence as it ridiculed you for becoming lost or uncertain of what to do, or scornful in your desire to get it right? Of course not; the sad part is we do all of those things ourselves.

Of the millions of species living on the planet we are the only ones who are so critical and judgemental about our perceived failings. We are totally unique in the way we look at ourselves, the way we live our lives and use this negative mind set when trying to achieve anything. We casually say 'you learn by your mistakes' but we only want this to apply to others. Our first reaction to making a mistake is usually to deny it, justify it or if caught out blame it on someone else. We see mistakes as flaws in our character, an indication that the person making them is in some way a failure. Conditioned from an early age in this negative way of thinking, we take on the role of the stern parent and become our severest critic, our own worst enemy not realising this undermines the possibility of any real achievement. When the negative outcome reflects the belief that helped create it, we congratulate ourselves on knowing how little we could achieve. Failure of any kind is an outcome; it's not an end result but an unwanted result. Successful people know that success comes out of failure. Failure to them has many names; they know it as practice, training, revision or reflection, trial and error or experience, and each of these is a form of education that moves the successful person along their chosen route until they eventually reach their destination. The successful outcome they desire.

Personal development is a process of learning new ways to do things. Releasing your grip on reality as you let go of the old and accept the new without judgement or criticism. We do what we do because that's what we know, and when we know different we do things differently. This knowledge can be taught, given or discovered, but we must find understanding within ourselves. Learning any new skill takes us into the unknown, we move out of our comfort zone and into the realms of uncertainty and more than a little confusion. If we want something different be it success, achievement or improvement then we must be willing and ready do something new to achieve it, for repetition serves to confirm the established and what is already known. A dead end or wrong turning is not a reason for personal criticism or rejection but a time of reflection and redirection. Each wrong turn, each door of opportunity that's tried and then closed takes us one step closer to our destination. We're not failing in our achievement, we are simply eliminating the options that don't work, reducing the number of obstacles that prevent us from achieving the result and the success we desire.

Chapter Forty-Four

In search of my elusive 'Ready'

When I want to do something I enjoy or excites me, ready is there before me. When it's something I dread or don't want to do my ready is nowhere to be found and I have to go it alone with only doubt and uncertainty for company. My ready is elusive and unreliable, and when waiting for it to arrive isn't an option, I must find the courage to take that step into the unknown.

Chapter Forty-Five

I Choose

'I choose' are two powerful and liberating words. In saying I choose we are making a statement of intent and recognising the power we have to shape our destiny. But before we can choose we must first accept there are choices to be made and where the responsibility lies. If I wish to understand and harness the power of my mind then I must first accept the greatest power is one which is measured and controlled in its use, and aware of the consequences of its own actions. The mind is no different and before we can fully understand what it means to say I choose we must first accept that we are the sole authors to our story and own the copyright for every thought we produce, either intentionally or by default. It is easier to tell ourselves that our thoughts 'just happen; it's our minds fault and we have little or no control over the flow of mental junk mail generated. As the old saying goes 'where ignorance is bliss, 'tis folly to be wise' and this lack of knowledge in the role we play allows us to find happiness in ignorance, because it is more comfortable not to know certain things, like where the body of truth is buried.

When we become aware knowledge and understanding begins to free us from the ties imposed by ignorance and fear, releasing us from the crippling feeling powerless, and the ensuing victim mentality. Raising our awareness is the key to personal development and sustainable change. Harsh self-judgment should never be an issue; berating ourselves for our lack of knowledge and understanding is symptomatic of the ignorance we need to let go of and leave behind. If we don't know or understand education not punishment is required. If we know but have momentarily forgotten then a gentle reminder will achieve far more than a torrent of self-abuse and criticism ever will. Once our ego can get over the fact that we have to take personal responsibility for the quality and quantity of our thoughts, the good, the bad and the indifferent, without self-destructing on some unnecessary and counterproductive guilt trip, we can begin to understand the true power in the words I choose. When choice is an option knowledge and understanding provide the power and opportunity to choose wisely. To choose thoughts which are positive, healthy and life affirming?

The most neglected relationship we have is the one we have with ourselves. The greatest challenge is to know the stranger that lives our life, and in the process claim ownership and mastery of our mind. To claim ownership of the thoughts we think, the beliefs they help to form, and the reality they must ultimately create. Like the servant given power and responsibility beyond their capabilities the mind can prove to be a terrible task master, but with loving guidance and correction can be the most attentive and loyal servant. Mistakes do not make us a bad person; they make us human and provide us with the opportunity to learn, develop and grow, but a mistake made often is no longer a mistake, it's a personal choice disguised as a habit, that must bring with it consequences. Skills and abilities take time, commitment and practice to hone to the point of mastery of the mind.

A power that is measured and controlled, and aware of the creative consequences of its actions. Ignorance is a blanket that covers us, comfort sedates the will, but on wakening the words 'I choose' free us to take personal responsibility for the life we create and wish to live, one thought, belief and experience at a time.

Chapter Forty-Six

A new improvement formula .... just so you don't have to

As much as we would like it to be otherwise, personal development is an inside job. No manner of quick fixes will work if we haven't first accepted personal responsibility to what's going on in our lives. Until we make that important connection between our thoughts, the beliefs they create, the experiences we have to live through on a daily basis, we will continue to look for an external solution to what is an internal problem. An internal problem that first must be addressed before any meaningful development can take place.

Failure to do so can result in a misplaced desire to attend the next workshop, seminar or retreat in order to find that illusive moment of enlightenment, failing that, train in the newest healing modality that's just arrived on the personal development market place. We are encouraged to believe we are broken and others hold the key to our recovery, all we have to do is keep looking until we find the right product that 'resonates' with us, spend our money, sit back and wait for the magic to happen.

Contrary to popular belief personal development and the healing it brings isn't always a nice and enjoyable experience. Sometimes we need to go through a detox as we struggle to let go of the crap in our lives, ready to receive the good stuff. This goes some of the way to explaining why we prefer to go for what appears an easier option. If anything or anyone offers us a miracle cure no matter how expensive, it has to be better than having to do all the work ourselves. But if there is a real need for you to develop and grow, it's safe to assume a degree of ignorance and fear are present at some level requiring knowledge and understanding to be brought to bear. Without it personal development and the healing it brings is impossible. A large number of today's illnesses and diseases have their root cause in our sedentary and unhealthy life styles, the poor life choices we make on a daily basis. Healing and personal development not only demand change, it also requires us to re-evaluate our lives and question both our motives and actions to understand what we are doing, and why. But if you challenge a person's deep seated beliefs, you are also challenging the core values of the person who holds them to be true. If their life has been built upon a set of beliefs, values and principles that are negative and self-destructive they will find the thought of having to dismantle them stressful, and the idea of change more than a little frightening.

Healing and personal development are big business and in many ways it's our inability or unwillingness to take responsibility for a little personal in house cleaning, has helped make it a commodity and a marketable product. A product branded and rebranded to keep it fresh and contemporary, packaged and marketed to create a high profile and attract new clients who are looking for 'enlightenment'. There is nothing wrong in seeking help and guidance when we need to; it shows you are aware of an issue that needs to be resolved. There is nothing wrong in others providing a service to help others and charge a reasonable fee for their time and experience, but that help and guidance in whatever form it takes must empower the individual to take responsibility for their own life. Primary care begins with us and when it comes to personal development we are *'primus inter pares'* first among equals; the senior member committed to the healing and development of self. When we fail to accept personal responsibility for our health and wellbeing; we fail to acknowledge the link between the choices we make and the life we lead. We disempower ourselves and compound the situation even further. In handing over our hard earned money, we must remember to retain our personal responsibility and duty of care for our health and wellbeing. It's our life and only we can live it, putting right what needs to be corrected.

If we are not careful our commitment can be reduced to the level of a magical cleaning product. *'For a limited time only, at a special introductory price. Our new and improved formula is guaranteed to get rid of 99.9% of all known problems. It's tough on fears and is powerful enough to cut through all of those blemishes and imperfections. It's easy to use, and does all of the hard work so you don't have to'.* Terms and conditions apply. Terms and conditions are restrictions, and the small print is small for a very good reason, what is harder to read is harder to understand, and the devil is hidden in the detail. We should always take the time to read the label and the small print to make sure we know exactly what we are buying into, and what if anything we can hope to get out of it. No person or product no matter how great has the power to change our lives without our co-operation, and we should never under value the power we possess to develop ourselves in order to realise our full potential.

Chapter Forty-Seven

A little knowledge can be a dangerous thing

Knowledge begins as simple thought; the seed of an idea sown in a fertile mind that takes root and grows. The acquisition of knowledge and understanding requires the acceptance of the new, letting go of beliefs we have outgrown or no longer reflect the person we have become. Sometimes knowledge and understanding asks us to reject what we once held firmly as truth. In doing so the old is swept away in order that a solid foundation can be laid down, upon which to establish a new belief system.

A closed mind is unaware of its own ignorance, a prisoner of its own rigid beliefs. Ignorance keeps us trapped within a comfort zone defined by the realms of the unknown and the things we fear the most. Change is dangerous and threatens to set us free from the confines ignorance provides. Change is only possible when we are prepared to question what we hold to be true, but forced to accept a belief against our will we revert back to our old ways at the first opportunity and seek sanctuary behind the walls built to keep the 'dangerous' unknown at bay.

Chapter Forty-Eight

The future is a child in time;
already conceived, but not yet born.

It's human nature to want to put as much distance between ourselves and anything we want to release or get rid go of, but no matter how much we wish to separate ourselves from the past we can't. The past is as much a part of us as the present moment, and the future are. The past is the parent to the present moment; the future is the child in time, already conceived but not yet born.

If we see the past as an adversary who must be fought in order to gain a foothold on our future then the battle will be never ending. The greatest foe we face is ourselves, and this internal power struggle has the potential to destroy us if we let it. The past didn't just happen it was created and it has as much right to exist as the present and the future, it will not, and cannot be denied. The pain we sometimes experience is not from the past itself but the conflict that comes from our reluctance to acknowledge the past was instrumental to the creation of the person we have become.

In many ways the past is the teacher that presents us with the lesson in the here and now. If we are wise enough to learn from it the future becomes the truth demonstrated. The past once created cannot be undone, but it can become worn by the passage of time and our many visits. Every time we revisit the past we leave a piece of ourselves there, and bring the residue of the past into the present moment thus strengthening the very bonds we wish to break. Time presents us with an opportunity to move on, a chance to gain perspective if we would just acknowledge the debt we owe to our past, and make peace in order that the fragmented self can be made whole. It is impossible to heal the self without having the willingness and the desire to love and forgive oneself for past mistakes and perceived imperfections. The guilt we hold on to does not come from love. Guilt is the ego's way of exerting dominance and control, like a vengeful domineering parent figure that must be obeyed at all times.

274

Freedom and healing comes when we accept that no one out ranks us when it comes to the authority of ourselves, we are the undisputed and powerful CEO of Self Inc.

The greatest weapon to be used against anyone is the power of their own ignorance. The negative ego is a past master at using our ignorance and fear to make us believe we are powerless and deserving of punishment for past mistakes. If no one is available to punish us, in our ignorance we are more than happy to take on that responsibility. In the process, inflicting punishment on ourselves that is disproportionate to the perceived 'offence' and is neither deserving, nor required. We are born into an imperfect world with the (soul) purpose to learn, develop and grow. The desire for perfection is at odds with the task at hand which is to make mistakes, to learn from them and in doing so develop physically and spiritually. Success without failure teaches us nothing. We celebrate success giving little thought to the process that brought about the achievement. Failure demands our attention and with it an inquisition as to what went wrong. Lacking knowledge and understanding we can allow negativity to raise its ugly head with the need to blame and hold someone accountable, with an ensuing guilt trip that can last a life time.

Letting go does not require us to feel guilty or obligated to our past mistakes; guilt is a choice that is both destructive and counterproductive and serves no purpose other than self-imposed punishment and attachment to a past, real or imaginary. Letting go of the past requires us to be honest with ourselves and accept that mistakes were made. While ignorance covers a multitude of sins, it also encompasses a lifetime of experiences that demanded we make choices often without the life experience to do so, or realising the consequences of our actions.

We are not asked or expected to be perfect. We are simply asked to do the best that we can with what knowledge and understanding we have available to us at the time, and when we know better, to do better. Mistakes do not denote a bad person; they signify a work in progress whose faults when overcome stand not to devalue and diminish, but to praise the progress made and in recognition of the challenges to be overcome. Taking time to return to where it all began can with the right mindset can be a major part of the healing process. We are not there to dwell on the past but to draw a line under it and in doing so accept that what debt there was has been paid in full by the sacrifice of our peace of mind. We have come to make peace with our past, so that we are able to part on good terms, to live in the present, and create the future we desire.

Chapter Forty-Nine

It's easier to be real than perfect

You have a much better chance of being real than you have of being perfect. It will take less time and lead to a greater sense of personal achievement and happiness.

Chapter Fifty

Why do my mistakes have the loudest voice?

Why are my mistakes so outspoken while the good I have done remains silent in times when I need their support the most. Why do my past mistakes seem so intent on forcing their way into the present moment, while the good that I do hides out of sight and out of mind. Why is what I did at a time when I knew no better more important than actions now defined by knowledge and understanding? If our past mistakes are outspoken it's because we in our ignorance have empowered them to be so. Ignorance and fear would have us believe that we are subservient to our past and prisoner of our guilt without the chance of parole, even when the light of knowledge and understanding provides the key to our freedom. Burdened down with the belief in guilt and punishment we take on the roles of judge, jury and inquisitor, giving voice to our many failings and the belief in the 'bad' person who made them. Mistakes do not define a person good or bad. If we must sit in judgement then we must consider both the circumstances and the action taken for we are neither perfect nor imperfect, we are simply a work in progress. An error in judgement, a decision made when lacking knowledge and understanding to the true consequences of our actions does not denote a flaw in the design, or a lack of potential to achieve greatness.

Life is a great teacher to the willing student. Unfortunately, it tests us before we have the experience needed to know the answers, but in doing so our actions contain the lessons required to educate us. Mistakes are a sign of spiritual growth not a social deformity. A mistake often made is a decision not an accident, a decision that fulfils a deep-seated need that can be obscured by conditioning, ignorance and fear. Once we have journeyed to locate and understand the motivation of our actions come the responsibility to do better. We may aspire to reach higher but our actions are always grounded by our current level of awareness. As we raise our awareness we automatically raise our capacity for greatness which is then reflected in the quality of our actions. The way we treat others and more importantly the way in which we treat ourselves.

I no longer seek to silence the voice of my past mistakes for in doing so I dis-empower great teachers of their ability to educate me. Neither do I seek to bask in the glow of some unrealistic ideal for it's the ego that would have us believe that no good deed goes unpunished so it's better to stay silent about the good that we do. The moment we acknowledge the speaker we acknowledge their right to speak and the validity of the message they bring. In doing so we no longer see conflict between opposing factions once perceived as success and failure. With this shift in our perception we recognise them as coming from the same seed and the fruits of our labours at different stages of our spiritual growth. When we can acknowledge the true nature of our mistakes they have gained the recognition they deserve and no longer need to shout in order to get our attention. My good deeds in their wisdom kept their peace and waited patiently for the time when I was able to listen and understand what these great teachers were trying to tell me.

Their silence was never a form of rejection it simply created the space for me to grow and the realisation that some of the greatest lessons are found in silence if we are willing and able to listen.

Chapter Fifty-One

My windows may need cleaning

What we believe determines our reality; our beliefs create structure and conformity, a platform that forms a foundation of our very existence and to a great extent determines what we believe to be true, real, and acceptable. We see what we expect to see, and sometimes we see only what we believe to be possible. They say to see is to believe, but in reality, it's as much about believing before we can see. Our thoughts can be very powerful and persuasive, but when it comes to a fight between our thoughts and our beliefs there's no contest, our beliefs will win every time. To use a computer analogy our thoughts are like the cursor that moves across the screen, but our beliefs are the programs creating the work. The quality of that work is determined by the quality of the programmes, our ability to understand and work with them. Personal awareness is about understanding the negative programme we are running here and now, and how to upgrade in order to improve the quality of our most important piece of work; ourselves.

Chapter Fifty-Two

Some lessons are free, but others come at a price

We make a mistake, nobody gets hurt and no one notices. Embarrassed and relieved we can feel we got away with it. But do we come out of the experience wiser, or have we simply written it off as an unfortunate accident that could happen to anyone, and give it no more thought. In many ways a lesson is only a lesson when we realise the value of the experience before us and we have the presence of mind to accept it and learn from it. Having learnt the lesson we must then ensure this is reflected in the way we live our life from that point on. A 'mistake' repeated time and time again is no longer a mistake, it's a course of action that we have chosen to make regardless of the consequences to ourselves and those around us.

Even the most negative action serves a purpose. The experience is transformed into a lesson when we begin to think about what we are doing, why we are doing it, and what if anything we are getting out of the experience. Ignorance and fear hide a multitude of sins, misconceptions and misguided beliefs about what is possible, appropriate and acceptable. In short, the conditioning we have come to accepted over time without question. Lessons of any kind challenge what we hold to be true and ask us to open our mind to accept and apply a new and raised level of knowledge and understanding.

Lessons learnt provide us with experience, options and new found ability. Lessons that go un-noticed or unrecognised will simply be repeated time and time again until we do.

Chapter Fifty-Three

Searching for that elusive excuse

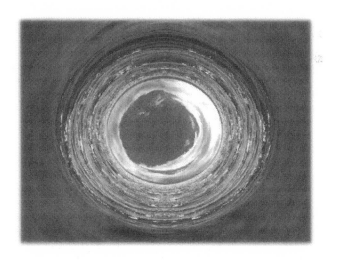

Excuses are wonderful things even when they don't exist. If you are looking for an excuse you will find one, it will appear out of nowhere as if by magic, tailor made to suit every occasion.

The one thing that never requires an excuse is the letting go of the things in life that cause us pain and suffering. The claiming of our self-respect and self-worth require neither excuses, justification or the approval of others, we simply have to master the use of the word 'no'. Such a small word yet so difficult to say when we continually sacrifice our happiness, health and wellbeing for the sake of others indifference to our suffering.

Chapter Fifty-Four

Your power of control

The most powerful form of control is that which goes unnoticed or accepted as the norm. To exist it requires our acceptance of the situation and ignorance of the chains that bind us. Knowledge and understanding and the enlightenment it brings are the nemesis of this subversive control and freedom can only be found beyond the limitations of our ignorance and fear. Freedom begins in the mind. Through the freedom of thought comes the ability to think and question everything, accepting only that which empowers and frees each one of us to become a seeker of truth.

Chapter Fifty-Five

Punishment and rewards are short lived

Reward and punishment have a very short shelf life and need to be renewed and updated on a regular basis to remain effective. Sustainable change becomes possible when education asks us to release our grip on reality, on what we hold to be true and embrace the unknown. If we want something different we must be prepared to do something differently in order to achieve it, but it's only when we know better, can we choose to do better.

Chapter Fifty-Six

Better to be freed by the truth than held captive by a lie

Lies can be wonderful things when their words are sweet to the ears and we have no desire to hear the truth. Lies make great companions when we seek to deceive or hide behind the actions that would otherwise reflect our true character. The most convincing lie is that which contains the greatest element of truth; it entraps the unwary as they hold onto what they wish to be true. In doing so, they unwittingly become prisoners of ignorance and fear. Truth is uncompromising; its hard edges can appear abrupt and unyielding, yet it is often the grain of truth that irritates us more than the words themselves. Lies must always be dressed to hide their true image; lies seek to conceal and confuse while the truth seeks to enlighten and educate. No matter how uncomfortable the truth is, it is better to be freed from ignorance and fear than held captive by a lie.

Chapter Fifty-Seven

Do we only value what we pay for?

Is it true we only value what we pay for or have we simply made it so by literally buying into this belief? We didn't always live in such a materialistic society, there was a time when exchange and barter were the accepted means of providing a product or service, and getting what you needed in return. There is nothing wrong with valuing your time, experience, and learning, but once you link it to your self-worth and self-esteem you have made yourself a commodity defined by a monetary value.

If this self-evaluation becomes rigid and inflexible you are setting limits on who are able to afford your help, and inadvertently allowing finance or the lack of it to become a barrier to another's personal development. If we have the power and desire to set a value on the work we do, then we must also have the power and the confidence to be able to decide the nature of the exchange rate without the fear that anything less than top dollar in some way cheapens us and devalues the service that we provide. Value is subjective; what is a trinket to one is treasure to another; money is an agreed bench mark as to what we perceive something is worth, but as any experienced salesperson will tell you value is defined by how much someone is willing to pay as by the product itself. When it comes to our personal evaluation emotional attachment can often affect our perception, none more so when it comes to establishing our self-worth for the first time.

Childhood and personal awareness share many similarities. In both we come from a place of not knowing and look to others to show us the way, in the process we accept without question the thoughts beliefs and values of those with the power to influence us. The must do's of childhood are often there to keep us safe and rightly so, but when it comes to our own development we should adopt a more measured and considered approach when faced with a whole range of must do's.

If I tell you, you must do something to make any form of progress this is simply my opinion, based on my own journey and life experiences, which are formed by my thoughts, beliefs and actions. This is my path not yours and we all have to break new ground and old beliefs in equal measure to find our own way. Development of any kind is personal and as such there can't be a one size fits all solution to enlightenment, it's your life and you alone have the duty of care, the responsibility to live it. All any teacher can do is share experiences and the knowledge and understanding it brings, the teacher can point the way but it's the student who must find their own path.

If we distil the concept of 'must do's' and reduce it to its most basic level there is only one 'must do' that remains constant and able to stand up to the most stringent analysis, and that is at all times ''what we must do is learn to think for ourselves''. Before there is anything to do there is always something to know and learn about ourselves and the choices before us. Tradition, age or authority doesn't own the monopoly on wisdom, and if we surrender our development to others, we have no one to blame but ourselves if we become lost, confused and disillusioned.

We never need to look for an excuse to change or ask another person for permission to develop and grow. We choose what defines us; we set the value of our self-worth and the service we provide, but if we equate who and what we are to nothing more than a monetary value we run the risk of segregating ourselves from those who can't afford us but need our help the most. In doing so we devalue our self-worth and our value as a person no matter how high we stand in the esteem of others.

Chapter Fifty-Eight

Change walks silently through life

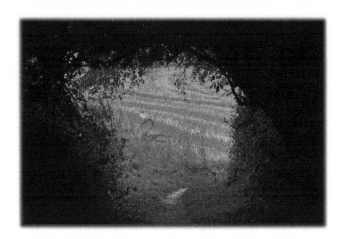

Change is a constant companion that often goes unnoticed as it walks silently through our lives. Caught up in the rush of life we give little thought to what passes us by, yet it's only when we look back we see how different things are and the changes that have taken place while we were absent from our life.

Change

Change cannot be divorced from life; it's the very fabric of life itself. Change can be evolutionary, or revolutionary, we must choose. Comfort is a sedative, which robs us of the will to change. Comfort is warm and secure. Change is uncomfortable, dangerous and uncertain. It is life.

Chapter Fifty-Nine

The only person we can heal is ourselves

A major precept of Reiki that is sometimes overlooked is the only person we can heal is oneself. When we read this part of the Reiki story it's a very clear and precise statement. There's nothing vague about it, it says quite simply and clearly 'the only person you can heal is you'. So where does this leave us as self-proclaimed healers of others? The truth is those eight little words don't leave us a great deal of room to manoeuvre and this is why they are sometimes ignored or misunderstood. They don't sit comfortably with the belief that Reiki gifts us all manner of healing abilities and that when Reiki attuned/empowered we are able to heal others. Unfortunately this is not the case. Before we precede any further let me state clearly and categorically that Reiki does work but not in the way that some believe it to. Purpose and meaning of any kind brings with it a point of reference; your actions must be in line with that point of reference in order to achieve your purpose or goal. Put simply a point of reference gives meaning, direction and context to what you do and the precept 'the only person we can heal is oneself' is a fundamental point of reference in Reiki.

Reiki is not and never has been about healing others, it's about you taking responsibility to heal yourself through the acquisition and application of knowledge and understanding Reiki can bring. I say can bring, because the student must take responsibility for their learning and not look to be spoon fed the information they require, or look to Reiki or anyone else to sort out all of your problems for you. Reiki is the teacher and healing is the educational subject matter. We must first change perceptions before we can change the physical reality. In doing so the unknown becomes known and knowledge becomes understanding.

The statement we can only heal ourselves is very clear and precise in several ways. Firstly it accepts that the process of healing is readily available to us all. Secondly it places the responsibility for our health and wellbeing fairly and squarely into the hands of each and every one of us. It does not say that something or someone else has the power to heal us; it is saying that we have both the power and the responsibility to heal ourselves by raising our level of awareness to the point where we can bring about the necessary changes in life, to create a state of health and wellbeing. We are born into this world with only two things guaranteed; our first and last breath and an indeterminate time between them to live our lives. In signing up for this earth while experience we and we alone must accept responsibility for the life we create once we reach a point of social maturity, when we decide to live by our own beliefs and values. In choosing to live by our own rules we must also accept the responsibility for our actions and the consequences they bring. For many of us those actions result in a state of illness and disease created by living in ignorance and fear. Ignorance in the true sense of the word lacking in knowledge and understanding and ignorant to the personal cost of the choices we make.

While contemporary medical science may not validate Reiki per se, what it does do is validate the Reiki precept of healing one self. Reiki and medical science are talking about the same reality, personal power and responsibility, and while we talk in terms of consciousness and raised spiritual awareness doctors use a more down to earth language. Theirs is easier to understand when trying to educate their patients to the lethal consequences of their sedentary life style. To the reality that obesity, diabetes and a large number of cancers and some mental health conditions are the result of our sustained use of alcohol, smoking and the negative life choices we make on a daily basis. These ailments, conditions and life choices are the modern day horsemen of the apocalypse. This is the reality that Reiki practitioners have to work with on a regular basis. Although we may not be aware of the causes we have to deal with effects that are presented to us in its many forms and guises. We may provide our attention and intention to help but its Reiki in the form of knowledge and understanding that brings a new perception to the recipient in order that they may begin the process of healing themselves. Because Reiki is consciousness in energy form, it's a distillation of knowledge and understanding that can work when the spoken word or a physical life experience has failed to resonate with the person in a life affirming way.

The evidence available is overwhelming and with the internet and communication technology freely available to everyone we can no longer use 'ignorance' as an excuse for our actions. We 'know' that negative life choices are dangerous to our health and will result in premature death and unnecessary suffering for many. But deep down we don't believe it will happen to us. If we did believe it we would live our lives differently, consciously affirming life each and every day through our thoughts and actions.

The emotions and actions our thoughts create have far reaching consequences. Our gene pool, our DNA the very fabric of our being is influenced, enhanced or adversely affected. This happens when our psychology becomes our biology through the quality of our thoughts and the attitudes and beliefs they create. *If we are the parent to the thought then the belief is the emerging adolescent and consequence is that thought fully grown.* A change in perception creates a new link and a new direction in the chain of events that is necessary to bring about a new life affirming reality. If we want something different then we must do something different to create it, for repetition does nothing more than reinforce what is already established.

Illness and disease as conditions require our participation; healing is about empowering people to take responsibility for their lives, to take ownership of the life they lead. Spiritual teachings speak of the healed having to take an active role in the healing process; a realisation that Dr Usui himself would eventually come to accept. But it's not about healing a condition in isolation without due consideration of the past, present and the future. Alleviating the condition is only one part of the healing process. It has to be viewed in context of the cause (the past) the condition (the present) and the remedial action taken (the future).

This is to ensure the cause and its ensuing symptoms are dealt with and a new perspective or positive mindset is in place so that the healing is comprehensive and complete. If the root cause goes untouched then the condition has grounds to return. If a change in perception doesn't accompany a change in the physical condition then the healing may lack the mental discipline and the emotional stability it requires to sustain good health and wellbeing. To heal our self is to accept that we have a duty of care and a responsibility to live our lives in such a way that creates and maintains good health and wellbeing in mind body and spirit.

We do this through the recognition and acceptance that our thoughts beliefs and actions must be life affirming and compatible with the outcome we desire. With this comes the realisation the attaining and maintaining of good health is an ongoing daily process. Good health is never guaranteed to anyone, shouldn't be taken for granted or considered as someone else's responsibility. It's our life and we must live it. Live it in a way that recognises all healing no matter what the source comes to us through the acquisition and application of knowledge and understanding. In teaching us the only person we can heal is ourselves Reiki is asking us to recognise, accept and exercise the power we hold in our own hands.

Chapter Sixty

The mind body connection

A scientific fact and spiritual truth that supports one another is that our psychology becomes our biology, or put another way what we believe to be true becomes our reality in mind, body and spirit. Medical science refers to this process as the mind body connection where the quality of our thoughts and beliefs has a direct effect on our body health and well-being, and ultimately our life expectancy. Psychiatric research has proven beyond doubt the correlation between the quality of our thoughts and beliefs, and the quality health we experience. Those thoughts and the generated neurological and chemical impulses they create that bring about physical changes in our body. The Bible says 'whatever we believe in our hearts we will become' and many personal development books and teachers, make similar statements, but without necessarily explaining why. The above mentioned research goes some way to support the validity of these claims. This mind body connection is responsible for amongst other things the placebo effect in the use of prescribed medication.

It has also been attributed to dramatic cases of remission in terminal illnesses, and some cases reported as 'miracle cures'. The one thing that's certain is that the mind and body are not separate entities, they are connected and the quality of the thoughts we generate on a regular basis and the beliefs they help create provide the structure to the life experiences we then have to live through. Through our ignorance and fear we have come to believe that we are prisoners chained to our past and powerless to secure our own release from these debilitating beliefs.

The mind body connection underpins the fact that our point of control is always in the here and now and as such our thoughts can be changed at a moment's notice. But to do this we must take responsibility for our thought process and accept that our thoughts and beliefs don't just happen, we create them out of habit, conditioning, boredom and desire. We have the ability and right to think whatever we wish, but with that right we have to accept responsibility for the quality of the thoughts we create. When for whatever reason negativity becomes our 'default setting' it becomes easier to think of illness and disease or any negative experience as misfortune or bad luck. This victim mentality dis-empowers us and takes away any personal responsibility for our thoughts, beliefs and actions.

Louise Hay says of illness: '*All illness comes from a state of unforgiveness. Whenever we are ill, we need to search our hearts to see who it is we need to forgive, and the person thought or belief you find it hardest to forgive release is the person or thing, you need to let go of the most*'. This statement may challenge our present beliefs, especially if we are struggling with a health issue that's causing us a great deal of suffering because no one wants to feel they are to blame for causing their own health problems. In releasing this situation it's important that we accept that blame is not an issue; we shouldn't blame ourselves for what we do out of ignorance or fear, lacking knowledge and understanding. We have a responsibility to educate ourselves to the implications and effects of our thoughts, beliefs and actions on our health and wellbeing.

We then need to take the steps necessary to improve the quality of our own lives, instead of giving that power to others in the mistaken belief that they have more control over our lives than we do. Healing is neither magical nor mystical; it's a process that requires steps to be taken to bring about the changes we desire. All healing comes from knowledge and understanding and the miraculous is a technology waiting to be discovered when we are willing and able to raise our level of awareness and embrace it.

Our body has the ability to heal and regenerate itself if we allow it to and don't impede its progress through the introduction of toxic thoughts and beliefs. Our thoughts and beliefs create our experiences; they not only create our reality they also create our perception of that reality. We create an experience then decide whether that experience is good or bad. Unlike us our body never lies. With its innate intelligence it links the energy of our thoughts and beliefs and the corresponding feelings and emotions they generate to the organs and functions of the body that resonates with that energy. Positive and negative thoughts, beliefs, feelings and emotions affect us at a cellular level and have the power to activate or immobilise our auto-immune system. To keep us healthy or sow the seeds of illness and disease, whether those seeds develop and grow, depends on how much time energy and attention we give to their cultivation, and the growing conditions we provide for them. Healing of any description comes through knowledge and understanding, and Reiki like education first opens the mind so that the body can change through the effects of raised awareness. Reiki is a teacher that educates first and foremost and asks us to challenge our perspective on life, to look at things differently and to accept new ways of thinking.

It asks us to let go of the old when we have outgrown it, and release those things that no longer support who we are or the person we wish to become. It can be a painful process, but this is always in relation to our resistance to letting go and fear of the unknown. Our thoughts are nothing more than mental energy in the form of focussed attention and intention, and as such can be changed in an instant. Procrastination is the nemesis that silently erodes the time we have, and comfort is the sedative that robs us of the will to venture beyond that which we already know. There is nothing new to be found in the sedentary lifestyle of our comfort zone, the new always lies beyond the limitations we have set ourselves. The greatest challenge we face is to find the courage to dismantle the barriers that create a false sense of security. To challenge in equal measure the old and the new, what we have grown used to and what we now hold to be true. As the old proverb says *'you will come to know the truth, and the truth will set you free'*.

Chapter Sixty-One

The healing power of happiness

A major precept of Reiki is that the only p erson we can heal is ourselves. This is achieved through a change in perception and through the acquisition and application of knowledge and understanding. Without it there can be no healing, be it of mind, body or spirit. In healing oneself we are given the opportunity to learn the lessons necessary that enable us to help others heal themselves. In truth every Reiki practitioner is a facilitator of knowledge and understanding regardless of the degree of expertise they have achieved.

Self-healing is much more about changing our perception than changing a physical condition, for one is a prerequisite for the other. As co-creators we give meaning to the experiences we live through this is why there is no standard response to any given situation or experience. People feel and deal with things differently and a change in perception leads to a change of values, and a growing understanding of what's happening and why. The healing process may still be physically or emotionally painful but it becomes a pain with purpose and meaning as through this change in perspective we recognise it for what it is, working through it in order that it can be released and let go.

On this personal journey fear and regret are often our travelling companions. Regret is the one who is always lagging behind; it tries to get us to turn back, to turn around and focus on the past. It constantly reminds us of whom and what we once were, regret like a scornful parent is ever dismissive of what we have achieved, how far we have travelled, the changes we have made and the person we have become. Regret tells us that the success and happiness we seek have to be earned and we do not deserve it because of who we are and the mistakes we have made. Fear unrestrained runs ahead of us, it lays in wait ready to jump out and sabotage our progress when we least expect it.

Fear creates the illusion of barriers where none exist and leads us to believe that our path is fraught with hazards and pitfalls, with every shadow concealing dangers ready to bring any progress to a premature end.

Happiness can only be experienced in the moment; the present moment, for this is all the time we have. If we continually focus on the past or the future we deny ourselves the opportunity to create the happiness we desire in the here and now. Problems arise when we link our happiness to the achievement of goals instead of focusing on the creation of happiness itself. In doing so we convince ourselves that happiness is the result or by-product of an external experience instead of an internal creative process. Happiness is a state of mind; a thought process that elicits an emotional response which then creates a physical sensation and ultimately an external experience. Through the power of our thoughts our psychology becomes our biology and directly affects our health and well-being. Every thought will find a way to express itself; thoughts that if sustained will go on to create our beliefs and eventually the reality we must experience.

When happiness is linked to attainment we are sending out the message that we can't be happy in the here and now, in the present moment because our happiness has to be earned and will only be achievable if we are talented, able gifted or worthy enough to receive it. All of these thoughts are negative based self-judgements that promote the idea that happiness is 'out there' somewhere waiting to be discovered, instead of an internal experience waiting to be created. By attaching happiness to the acquisition of things or the achievement of goals we are saying that our happiness has to be put on hold until the achievement of those goals brings about the happiness and sense of achievement we desire. Any delay or even failure to achieve those goals can result in disappointment, and a sense of failure which can then trigger feelings of inadequacy, low self-esteem. In some extreme cases the onset of depression, illness and disease through the suppression of our immune system. Many people already know from personal experience that getting upset or angry can raise their blood pressure. Some have found to their cost that if anger or aggression has become their 'default response' their immune system is suppressed to such an extent it can over time, result in the onset of ill health, heart disease and strokes.

If negative thoughts and emotions have an adverse effect on our health and wellbeing, then positive thoughts and emotions such as joy and happiness can provide a measurable antidote. They effectively boost our immune system, lower our blood pressure and drastically reduce the risk for cardiovascular disease. Our thoughts and the emotions they create have far reaching consequences; our gene pool, our DNA the very fabric of our being is influenced, enhanced or adversely affected when our psychology becomes our biology through the quality of our thoughts and the attitudes and beliefs they create. While the adverse effects of negative thoughts and emotions are well documented there are a growing number of studies that now confirm that success doesn't lead to happiness, happiness actually leads to success and has measurable benefits to our health and wellbeing.

Pioneering work in this field of medicine is provides growing evidence that when people who are in a distressed state of mind are able to create or induce a feeling of, contentment, joy or happiness it has a positive and measurable effect to their health and wellbeing, and leads to amongst other things a quicker recovery of normal heart function. It also noted that the simple act of smiling also has the power to lower blood pressure and induce a more rapid heart rate recovery. So while some say there is no evidence to show that Reiki works other studies have shown that something as simple as a compassionate or loving touch has a measurable positive life affirming effect. Maybe it's now time to re-evaluate the evidence available to us, or simply change our perception of what Reiki is and the way it works. When we say that Reiki helps us to heal ourselves we are using a very broad brushstroke generalisation that does little to explain the 'healing' processes involved. Knowledge and understanding of the benefits of happiness and other positive based thoughts can change our perceptions and take healing out the realms of the mystical and miraculous. Make it a technology that can be understood and then used by everyone to enhance their health and wellbeing.

Happiness and positive induced emotions not only boost our immune system but also *undo* the effects of stress and anxiety, therefore not only improving quality of life but also protecting our health and wellbeing. They enhance nearly every facet of our being, including work performance, health, marriage, friendship, creativity, confidence and energy. It has to be said that happiness is no magic bullet, but it's clear that it lengthens the odds of getting disease or dying young. While happiness might not by itself prevent or cure disease there is no doubt that positive emotions and enjoyment of life contribute to better health and a longer lifespan. Current health advice and guidance focuses on avoiding obesity, eating a balanced healthy diet, not smoking and getting plenty of exercise. With the change in our perception of what contributes to a healthy lifestyle maybe it's time to add being happy and avoiding chronic anger to this list. Martin Seligman, the father of Positive Psychology says *'The best therapists do not merely heal damage; they help people identify and build their strengths and their virtues, the strengths and virtues which function to buffer against misfortune and against the psychological disorders, that may be the key to building resilience'* and ultimately maintaining long term health and wellbeing. As Reiki practitioners we have a responsibility and a duty of care to empower people to take responsibility for their own health and wellbeing when it's right and appropriate for them to do so. Healing should never be shrouded in mystery or hidden by rituals and tradition.

Healing is more about education than it is about changing a physical condition for without knowledge and understanding there is nothing to stop illness manifesting. Fear and ignorance provides the ideal conditions for all manner of ailments, illnesses and diseases to take root and grow. Healing like any concept, spiritual or otherwise, must transcend theoretical discussion and become a real life experience to be lived and learnt from. Positive thoughts and the emotions they create have the power to transform.

Happiness as part of that process has the ability to improve our quality of life, protect our health and wellbeing and enhance many aspects of our lives including work, health, relationships creativity and self-confidence, whilst generally raising our energy levels. All of which is available to us without prescription, and it falls squarely within the realms of healing one self, which is after all what Reiki is asking us to do.

Chapter Sixty-Two

Take time to be silly; it could be the most spiritual thing
you do!

A healthy life is about balance and harmony; put simply it's about fulfilling our duty of care to ourselves and to others. If we aspire to be a spiritual person, someone who tries to live out their highest beliefs in a practical down to earth way, while dealing with the rigors of everyday life, we should also take time out from our meditation sessions, our crystals, Reiki and the self-development workshops to be *silly*. If spirituality is one point of balance then childlike 'silliness' is the other.

The word 'silly' carries with it some negative connotations but if we look closely we see that the word also denotes being: *'carefree and lacking in serious purpose'*. But what greater purpose can there be than a carefree approach to our physical, emotional and spiritual wellbeing?

This need and desire is not childish, irresponsible, immature or foolish. It fulfils a childlike sense of wonder and sees the miracles in the mundane, it has a maturity that comes from the wisdom of innocence, and it recognises without judging how silly and self important we can sometimes be without realising it. It accepts responsibility and duty of care for our own health and happiness, it realises that you can't have one without the other for one is the counter balance to the other. It isn't afraid to laugh at itself, and recognises the wisdom of the fool. There is a time for all things, being silly in a childlike way is just as important as understanding the language of prayer or the finer points of spirituality. Each has its time and place and neither one stands higher than the other before God or the universe. A child sees the wonder in all things through eyes that haven't yet been clouded by ignorance and fear. For a child time stands still as it holds court with 'imaginary' friends as they discuss a magic kingdom we can no longer see. They see treasure in precious stones when all we see are pebbles; a puddle provides the opportunity to sail to distant shores and battle pirates and mythical monsters. We look into the same puddle and see the potential for dirty footprints on a kitchen floor. There is a time to be grown up and do the things that grownups do; a time to face the challenges of everyday life, but there is also a time to allow the child within us to rediscover the magic kingdom that we once knew.

There is a time for our physical and spiritual journey, but there is also a time to rest and play, a time to remember where we hid those golden shafts of sunlight that filtered through the trees on warm summer days; we instinctively knew they were precious and contained magical powers. Now is the time to rest for a short while, to play and rediscover those treasures you buried so long ago. You stand before the door to that lost kingdom, and silliness is the key.

Chapter Sixty-Three

Keeping life simple

It seems inherent in human nature to make things complicated. We take the simple things in life and make them unduly complex and more difficult than they need to be. It's almost as if we distrust simplicity and automatically presume that there must be more to 'it' than meets the eye. Maybe it's because we are born with love as our default mechanism but learn to fear and mistrust to such an extent it becomes second nature. Our approach to spirituality is no different. The more important we perceive a thing to be the more serious we become in its pursuit and in doing so we can lose perspective and objectivity and adopt the rigid mindset that something so profound must be complex and esoteric.

There are those who actively feed this myth by taking something simple, making it appear complex and complicated only to charge considerable amounts of money for the pleasure of making it 'easy to understand'. This is also the basic principle of 'rebranding' where a product goes full circle usually with a new name; new packaging in order to attract new customers to what is an old tried/tired and tested product. We see this in all things spiritual with people coming forward with a new spin on a very old idea, and it doesn't come much older that creation itself.

Reiki provides us with an excellent example of how a basic practice can give birth to countless derivatives. On close inspection are separated only by the front cover of the manual that carries its name and the obligatory symbols that try to create a sense of uniqueness, which on closer inspection is superficial or non-existent. Even if you factor in the differences between the Eastern and Western versions of the Reiki story and strip away the 'packaging' that is used in some cases to add volume and make it look more than it is, you are left with three very simple principles upon which everything else hangs. Unconditional love is the spiritual energy that forms the basis of all creation. Our free will is the means of all physical and spiritual growth, and this creative spiritual energy follows our intent to literally form our reality.

In Reiki as in many things in life 'less is more;' which when you think about it is the simplification of our actions. We do less until we reach the point where nothing appears to be happening yet everything that needs to be done is done through the power of our intent.

Dr Usui's memorial stone carries the inscription that his desire is for our Reiki to be 'formless and free flowing'. This can only happen when we let go of the many physical and mental trappings that can restrict its flow and impede our Reiki practice to such an extent that we become bogged down by techniques and procedures that provides rigidity and structure, and comfort in the knowledge, what is seen to be done provides visual 'proof' that something is happening.

All of the techniques, hand positions and symbols used in Reiki work for no other reason than they are all underwritten by the principle that energy must follow our intent. Read any book on the use of Reiki symbols and techniques and you will invariably find the link between the symbols and the catalytic power of our intent. Dr Usui would regularly empower/attune his students when they were nowhere near him, he was able to do this because he understood and accepted the spiritual law of intent. He had no need or desire to do anymore than was absolutely necessary to achieve the desired outcome. If we need proof we need look no further than science to validate this principle. Quantum physics provide the mathematical equations, which are a prerequisite to scientific study, and research based proof all energy, spiritual and physical is responsive to the conscious mind and instrumental to the creative process. There is nothing wrong with using symbols, hand positions or well documented techniques in our Reiki practice; they all work by nature of our intent. The level of their success will be defined by the quality and quantity of our intent, the recipient's receptivity to Reiki and the effect of the above principles.

Reiki as we know it is energy pure and simple; all else are nothing more than add-on's to try and give form to the formless. The danger comes when we begin to believe that the hand positions, symbols and techniques are Reiki and must be used 'religiously' in a pre-determined way in order for it to work. If the ultimate goal is for Reiki to be formless and free flowing; then the acceptance and application of unconditional love as the energy of creation, and the use of our intent, should be the only prerequisite to our practice, formless and free flowing, simplicity itself.

Chapter Sixty-Four

When the principle gets lost in the practice

Certain principles of Reiki are very clear and precise, there is no ambiguity and the wording is very specific in order to provide guidance and direction to our practice. One such principle is that the energy we call Reiki will *'go where it's needed and not where the recipient may want it to'*. Simple and straight forward; unfortunately simplicity has a tendency to be overlooked and undervalued, and human nature being what it is, even the most gifted practitioner can make the mistake of losing sight of this simple principle amid the complexities of their practice.

Let us take a moment to revisit the principle and view it in its simplest form, *'It goes where it's needed'*, There is no mention here about hand positions, the use of symbols, advanced techniques designed to enhance its effect, or the use of preparatory meditative practices to help us get into the right state of mind. *It goes where it's needed,* nothing more and nothing less. If we accept this principle then we must consider for a moment the how and why it is able to do so.

The ability to go only where it's needed reflects the presence of a higher level consciousness, put simply it knows stuff that we don't know matter how clever, experienced or intelligent we may appear to be, or think we are. Where our attention is drawn to the physical, mental or emotional symptom, this energy goes right to the source. In many cases the practitioner and recipient are unaware of what the cause may be, or misguided in the belief as to what's wrong with them.

Healing of any description is only possible through the acquisition and application of knowledge and understanding, so we come to realise that education plays a major part in the healing process. Healing requires us to understand the relationship between the underlying cause of illness and disease and the symptoms we then experience. Simply removing the symptom as if by magic is dangerous and serves no purpose other than to keep the person ignorant to the part they must play in the healing process. A condition that is created in error will be repeated unless the cause and the lack of knowledge and understanding which helped create it is addressed. Healing is never complete until it has reached the mind, body and spirit. The symptom or the condition which we can be seen is not the cause.

This lies at a much deeper level, at a cellular level and beyond. Energy's chosen method of transportation is vibration and frequency. Our thoughts and beliefs in the form of a mental representation have the power to affect those vibrations and frequencies in a positive or negative way.

When healing energy is introduced it has the power to literally go straight to the heart of the matter and effect a change in both the cause and the effect. First it educates then it helps bring about changes that reflect the healing process taking place. Help should never dis-empower. To help is to assist, support and empower, first with the belief then with the ability to stand alone. If the principle is correct then our practice should be in line with the principle. If the principle is simplicity itself, then so should our practice be, If not we should ask the question 'why not'. If it goes where it's needed then how it is introduced becomes secondary, which should lead us to question and separate our practice from the cosmetics and complexities that have become associated with many forms of healing. These things may have a place but in understanding the principle we must come to recognise what our practice presents to the world, and more importantly what it says about us.

Chapter Sixty-Five

Character, your spiritual Sat-Nav

Ok we all know about Reiki; it's well documented and in some cases, has been talked to death. On the other hand the subject of *'stuff'* by comparison is virgin territory that can, on closer inspection turn up a few new insights to the relationship between Reiki and stuff in general. Reiki in our life is a personal choice whereas stuff is a given. We are born into it, and start to collect it from the moment we enter into this big wide world, and if that wasn't enough, if you believe in reincarnation and karma we come with our flight bag and baggage already packed from one life to the next. Which if you think about it makes some sense as one experience can never be totally separated from its neighbour. What we experience in one moment inevitably affects how we view and respond to the next, so even if we don't have total recall we may well re-enter the world as a weary if not wise spirit, and far less pristine than we first imagine. How many of us have looked into the eyes of a baby and seen something that made us think or even say 'this child has been here before.'

So what is this stuff that appears at times almost magnetic in its ability to be drawn to us and cling to us like glue. Put simply stuff is baggage we collect and carry around with us throughout our lives. It can take the form of beliefs, fears phobia's, misguided responsibility misconceptions, anger, frustration and guilt, in short it's anything that impacts on the way we live our lives and affects the decisions we make. Children may be old spirits but when they enter this world they are governed by all of the laws of creation.

From the first moment of life they become aware of, listen to, accept and take responsibility for all manner of stuff without question. With their 'limited' knowledge and understanding they automatically assume they are the creators of their universe and take personal responsibility for many things. If mammy and daddy are upset, angry, sad or unhappy, fighting and hurting each other, or worse still hurting the child, in their mind they must be at fault and have done something wrong to create the situation.

The child automatically accepts its role in life's creative process albeit for the wrong reason. As we grow older we relinquish the idea possibly because of negative experiences that have 'proven' to our inexperienced minds that as children we have no control over life.

It's a lesson later in life that we must re-learn as we come to understand that through the very laws of creation we are the creator of our life experiences. Our thoughts are the architects and our beliefs good or bad are the builders that create the reality, the stuff we come experience in our lives. Some of the stuff we take on board isn't even our own. It belongs to those who decided to bring us into the world and became our parents, teacher's mentors and in some cases tormentors. But those who exert control over our development can only teach us what they themselves have learnt. Potentially some of the stuff we accept as our own can be nothing more than an established handed down family heirloom going back generations.

Because we know no better and we trust and love those who gave us this belief or value, we accept it as gospel and take it as our own. It then becomes part of the foundation that we build our life and experiences upon.

There is an old and some would say wise saying; 'when you meet the parents you can forgive the child anything'. However there comes a time in everyone's like when they begin to exercise their own free will, if we then suffer because of the consequences of our own actions, we must begin to let go of the victim mentality and start to take personal responsibility. We can use our upbringing as an excuse for our actions, or motivation to break the chain of events. I am because of this, or I am in spite of this. Taken to the extreme some negative stuff can lead us into some very dark and desolate places. Places where intolerance, abuse and suffering exist, but a closed dark mind is unaware of its own ignorance. Ignorance in the truest sense of the word, lacking in knowledge and understanding and the lightness of mind body and spirit that clarity can bring into our lives.

So having touched on stuff where does Reiki come into the equation and what's its relationship to our own stuff. Trust me if you are alive and reading this, the first is a pre-requisite for the second, you will have stuff in your life, and I can guarantee that some of it you won't even be aware of yet. The scary thing is it's the unknown stuff that exerts the greatest influence over all of us. Your belief in Reiki may even be part of the stuff you will need to revisit to see if you want to continue carrying this particular piece of luggage. Your Reiki study as baggage! It can be depending on what you believe and the expectations you may have about it.

There is a popular mis-conception that Reiki is a miracle cure all that comes into your life, takes over and does all the hard work for you based on what is defined as your 'higher good'. It can't, it never has and never will purely and simply because it has neither the power nor the authority to do so. By the very fact that Reiki exists within the realms of creation it can't operate arbitrarily outside of the laws that were instrumental in its creation. What it can and does do is work with us; education is the only means to establish sustainable change in anyone's life. Reiki educates us through the raising of our knowledge and understanding to the true nature of our own stuff, and the ways in which we can accept it, acknowledge it, learn from it and then move on. Lighter in mind body and spirit because of the baggage we have chosen to put down because we have outgrown it, or it no longer represents the person we have become.

Often quoted but not necessarily understood is the precept that the 'only person we can heal is ourselves' and spiritual teachings speak of the physician being commanded to 'heal thy self'. The emphasis is on the pivotal word of 'we' and not Reiki. If we are lacking in the knowledge and understanding to do so Reiki will help us to recognise, accept deal with and learn from our stuff in order that healing can take place. We can't even hide behind the 'higher good stuff' because we mistakenly come to believe that higher good equates to all things nice and wonderful.

The reality is totally different. The things we don't want to face about ourselves, the actions that may be at odds with the spiritual ideals we wish others to associate us with. Our relationships that may be abusive and self-destructive and all manner of issues we would prefer to lock away and pretend they don't exist. These are all in our highest good to accept and deal with. Anyone who has experienced these kinds of issues in their lives' will know how painful, frightening and debilitating it can be to face up to and address them. We can lie to others, we can even lie to ourselves but our body is always listening, it knows where all the stuff and truth is hidden, and our body never lies. It is the physical frame that holds the mirror showing us our true reflection of what's held within.

Think of Reiki as a very powerful guide, friend and mentor who never judges or imposes their will or their knowledge and understanding upon you. They will walk with you and when it's appropriate, help you to carry your load. They will never rob you of your power to choose or the ability to stand on your own feet, to deal with your own stuff no matter how painful or frightening it may at first appear. Strength comes through the exercising of our physical, mental emotional and spiritual muscles, dealing with adversity not hiding in another's shadow no matter how spiritual it or they may be. Knowledge and understanding is nothing more than an internal realisation to an external stimulation. Another more contemporary analogy would be to consider Reiki as your spiritual sat-nav. It will advise and guide you, it will show you the shortest route, and even give you the head's up on possible problems ahead on your journey. You are always in control and can at any time choose ignore its advice, or switch it off all together.

Reiki has helped me transform my life beyond all recognition. It has educated and empowered *me* to make the necessary changes that allowed love, healing knowledge and understanding to come in my life. It has shown me that God/Universe can only give us bigger and better things if our hands are free to take hold of them, and we have created the space in our lives and the mind set to receive them.

Part of my baggage is that I carry the historical title of Reiki Master but I can honestly say I haven't mastered anything nor will I this side of life. I'm simply a work in progress carrying the same baggage as you on my own personal journey. On good days I may even get to put stuff down that I don't need anymore, but after all this time in my rush to get where I'm going wherever that may be, I still occasionally make the mistake of picking up other people's stuff thinking it's my own. On reflection I guess I'm still just a student by another name, but you know what, it's just my stuff and I'm ok with that.

Chapter Sixty-Six

In search of the sacred

It has been said that religion is for those who don't want to go to hell whilst spirituality is for those who have already been there. Be that as it may, for anyone who sets out on that particular journey spiritual development has to be more than an intellectual exercise. To be of value it must transcend the written word into meaningful action, the concept of spirituality, of being a spiritual person must go beyond philosophical debate or high self-esteem and form the basis of who we are and how we live our lives. We need to make the connection between the spiritual and the physical; time spent developing our 'spirituality' is wasted if we don't reflect this new found knowledge in our everyday life. It's not enough to just talk the talk; we must also be willing and able to walk the walk, if we improve our minds we must ensure that this in turn is reflected in all other aspects of our lives.

Spirituality by definition is 'searching for the sacred' be that studying Reiki, faith in a religious deity, or simply becoming aware our higher self. Either way it isn't to be found in books, crystals, meditation, or native cultures, it's found in the heart mind and actions of the person seeking it. It's an internal process that should create an external experience. If we aren't careful we can lose track of what we are trying to achieve, and buy into the illusion of what we perceive a spiritual person to be. We create an image of change that lacks real substance, while convincing ourselves of our own spirituality. The danger lies in trying to become something other than ourselves in the mistaken belief that we are unworthy of enlightenment as we are. We believe we must change into this image of spirituality, and it's this image that is always at odds with the reality of whom and what we are.

Spiritual development is about a personal change in perspective that makes us a better person in the real world; it's not about a change of identity or hiding our true selves behind a veneer of spiritual superiority. It's not about becoming anything; it's not about trying to *do* spiritual things, it's about *being* ourselves in the here and now. It's about unconditional love for ourselves as we are warts and all, love for others as they are, and the planet that gives us life. As the ancient Benedictine prayer says; *'Lord thank you for revealing my true self to me, no matter how beautiful that may be'* Amen.

Living in the physical world as we do, our spirituality has to be practical and applicable to dealing with the challenges of everyday life. Once we discover this truth within ourselves we will see it reflected back to us in all aspects of life and we begin to see miracles even in the mundane. In our desire to get 'there' where ever that may be, we lose sight of living life and being in the here and now. Many spiritual disciplines teach us not to chase after something that can't be caught, the faster we chase after enlightenment the faster it recedes, like the distant horizon the harder we try to get there, the further away it appears. Spiritual maturity is about self-exploration through self-acceptance, trying to find out who we are, while having the ability to value and appreciate the things we discover about ourselves and others in a non-judgmental way.

The basis of all spirituality is unconditional love; and a person who grows in spiritual maturity seeks to apply this principle to their everyday life in a practical and down to earth way.

Our quest for spiritual awareness should never seek to remove us from the rigors of life for it's in those moments of adversity that life gifts us the opportunity to lay a mile marker to how far we have progressed on our journey of personal discovery. Part of this self-realisation is we are loved unconditionally, judgment is never an issue, and we should never judge others as a means of raising our own self esteem. We are loved unconditionally for no other reason that we exist as part of creation, we don't need to do anything to earn this love. We are, only because it is. High ideals must have their roots established in reality, our eyes may be looking to the heavens but our feet must be on solid ground. The way we live our lives, the way we treat ourselves and others, should reflect the spiritual truth that lives within us.

Chapter Sixty-Seven

The part we have to play

The path to understanding is very rarely if ever paved with gold; more often than not it's a journey of hardship and compromise, a path forged out of necessity and only made possible by the steps that we are willing to take. It's this journey of discovery that we call life and not a particular destination that provides us with the answers we seek. With birth and death as our parameters we are instilled with a sense of urgency and the belief 'time waits for no man'.

This urgency creates impatience and a desire for instant results and a prescriptive one size fits all solution to our problems. Yet in many cases progress is perceived to be slow and laboured when we compare it to our desire for answers. We want the answers now without really understanding the questions that we ask, and as the song goes *'there are more questions than answers, and the more I find out the less I know'*. Progression is defined as the process of developing gradually towards a more advanced state and by this definition we move from one level of awareness to another. But true progress must build on what has gone before. Being incremental and transitional it allows us to make sense of the processes and fit together the pieces in the jigsaw. As each piece of information comes together to be collectively known as knowledge and understanding, so a single footstep can claim its rightful place on the journey we call life. A problem we face when looking at the progress we have made is that we are limited to what we can see at any one time. A moment, minute, a day week or a year is nothing more than brief snapshots of our life at any given time. Although we may be able to look back with hind sight, what it gives in clarity it lacks in perspective for its difficult if not impossible to see the progress made retrospectively.

Yes we may remember individual highs and lows that can act as mile markers but the individual steps of our progress tend to be obscured and covered by the dust and debris of more recent experiences that grab and hold our attention. Yet paradoxically

346

it's only when we look back we are able to measure how far we have travelled. Reiki has taught me to take nothing for granted or automatically accept anything as gospel no matter what the source. The search for knowledge and understanding demands that we hold accepted wisdom and new truths up to the light of scrutiny even the Reiki story itself. Reiki can't exist outside of the laws of creation that brought it into existence. As new information emerges as it must, what we at this time consider a complete story simply becomes another chapter in the story of healing, and spiritual development.

History is a collection of stories written by those with the ability and power to do so. Human nature being what it is those who chronicled these events tended to enhance the role they played, to show they were motivated by the highest good regardless of the integrity of their actions. This has happened throughout time and continues today in all walks of life. Each and every one of us are guilty to one degree or another when it comes to the way we live our lives, the self-image we create for the world to see, and the motivation for our actions. History is a story and we are characters in this play we call life. Progress offers us the opportunity to play many roles; hero, villain, judge jury and in some cases our own executioner when through inappropriate life choices we reject knowledge and understanding to such an extent that illness and disease are created. Continuing with this analogy; Reiki takes the role of a wise and experienced mentor and coach, who asks us to step back from our performance and observe what is happening free from judgement or criticism. It also asks us to answer the age old actor's question 'what is my motivation for this role'.

With the answer come knowledge and understanding, and hopefully the ability to bring a deeper level of awareness, sensitivity and maturity to the role of parent, partner healer, teacher and friend, or whatever role we choose to play.

Progression is defined as the process of developing gradually towards a more advanced state and by this definition, we move from one level of awareness to another or from one role to another. In doing so it's important that we do so with an open mind free from criticism and judgement. Motivated by the desire for knowledge and understanding which forms the basis of healing for oneself and of one another. Our progress as individuals should always be kept in perspective. While our current level of awareness may be viewed as an advanced state in relation to those who have gone before us and on whose shoulders we stand, those who come after us may find us wanting in our limiting beliefs and actions. Better that we let go of judgement or misplaced self-satisfaction and accept that we are doing what we can and when we eventually know better we will do better. In this way, our progress becomes truth demonstrated.

Chapter Sixty-Eight

Please dial 1 for your wakeup call

When we think about improving our lives and changing things for the better, we invariably think of an increase in the 'good stuff' whatever we perceive that good stuff to be. With that comes a reduction in the 'bad' stuff as it's taken away by someone or something, or it just magically disappears. But if we take a moment to think about the reality of 'changing things for the better' we may come to realise there is more to it than we first thought. For things to change for the better we have to make the connection between our life and the person who lives it; we are the common denominator in every experience we have ever had. We are the sole tenant living in our body; we are the only thinker in our mind, the centre of our internal universe. Our life doesn't just happen it's created and we are both creator and narrator.

If we're not happy with the way things are then it's we who need to make some changes. If we want something different the first step is to start doing something different. This pivotal catalyst can be Reiki coming into our lives. Change requires choice, it also requires the belief that you are capable of change, and you have the desire or intent to bring about that change in your life. Change is not about sitting back moaning and waiting for someone else to sort out your problems for you, you are your problem and within every problem come the seeds to their solution. Albert Einstein once said 'a problem can never be solved by the same mindset that created it' if you want to find a solution to any problem you must first raise your level of awareness to gain a perspective that lies outside of the problem. You are the only one that can create the choice, through the belief and intent to bring about this change for the better.

You have to do something new, or let go of the old stuff. Reiki can be the catalyst that creates the ripple of dissatisfaction in your current state, either way development requires change and all development creates movement, you can't change and stay the same. Something will eventually have to give.

Our negative ego would have us believe that it knows best; it's much safer to stay the way you are, no matter how bad you think things are they will only get worse if you begin to interfere and try to change. It will try to make you believe that no good deed goes unpunished and that self-improvement comes from arrogance and not knowledge and understanding. If our higher self is the wise and knowledgeable teacher wanting only the best for us, our ego by comparison is the harsh selfish authoritative figure that has to be in control and obeyed at all times. From the negative ego's point of view, a change for the better would be no change at all. Things staying the way they are with lots of self-imposed limitations to hide behind, and the belief that nothing is ever our fault. Through the study of spiritual teachings we can begin to realise that our higher self doesn't look at things in the same way. It doesn't see fault or blame; it merely sees adverse effects brought about by

Blame and guilt don't exist for the higher self, they are illusions created by the ego as a means of maintaining control over us. The higher self wants us to take responsibility for our own actions and beliefs and enjoy the rewards that come through knowledge and understanding. From the higher self's point of view a change for the better would be the realisation that you are never isolated or alone. That you have access to a higher knowledge than the ego could ever imagine, you have the power to create the kind of life you wish to live. Reiki can provide the initial insight and the tools to bring about this change, but it won't do it for you because that's your responsibility.

Our higher self wants us to become aware of the harmful patterns that we keep repeating in our lives and the way we hurt ourselves through ignorance and fear. We need to let go of the past and the stuff we hang on to out of fear, habit or desperation. Unfortunately this won't just disappear, it has to be acknowledged resolved and then released, more often with professional help that lies outside the remit of Reiki. This change for better may not appear so when we are faced with issues we would prefer to ignore or pretend didn't exist. Change can be traumatic, but this is due in part to our attitude to change in general. Change takes us out of our comfort zone and into the unknown and we can view it as losing something we value, something to be taken away from us. It's because of this negative attitude we would much prefer to stay with the tried and tested no matter how unhealthy it may be, and in the process try to maintain the status quo by hanging on to stuff that is harmful and self-destructive. In this instance pain and suffering are always in relation to our resistance to change, the more we resist change the more traumatic the situation may appear to become.

That which exists must be governed by the laws that were instrumental in its creation. We are governed by the law of cause and effect; nothing happens by accident and nothing changes arbitrarily of its own accord. If we wish a situation to improve then we must play our part in bringing about the change we desire for even miracles must adhere to the laws of creation. There are no spectators in life only those who are asleep and those who are awake to this fact. A change for the better requires an understanding and appreciation of what we already have; it's this awakening sometimes through a spiritual induced wakeup call that can determine what we perceive to be better. It's this awareness, this knowledge and understanding which motivates us to bring about a change for the better, and in doing so the healing begins.

Chapter Sixty-Nine

How do we arrive at 'getting it right'?

The destination is only one part of our journey; with any journey we require a point of departure, a beginning, a point of reference before we can begin our journey. A starting point showing us where we are in relation to where we think we want to be, will determine the direction we need to take in order to reach our destination.

If we don't know where we are, or where we are going, how are we going to reach our destination? We may do no more than drift through life at the mercy of chance and circumstance, or stay rooted to the spot out of fear of being lost and alone. If on our journey of discovery 'getting it right' is our destination, then we must accept that we approach it from a place of not knowing and possibly getting it wrong. As we move towards our goal we move out of the darkness of ignorance and fear, and with this new dawning come the ability to see clearly and measure how far we have travelled. It's only by looking back can we truly measure our progress and how far we have come.

What we see and believe is defined by our standpoint at any moment in time; each new step forward gives us a different perspective, and a different point of view. Having arrived at our destination, we realise that not everyone may share our point of view. Not everyone makes their journey willingly and some fail to reach their destination. Of those who find their way to getting it right, not everyone will be happy or satisfied with the truth they find there. Sometimes we will be given the opportunity to rediscover new truths that have been lost in the mists of time; having reached our destination we may find ourselves alone for a short while, but our strength and determination to break new ground, gives courage to others to follow in our footsteps and make their own journey of getting it right.

Chapter Seventy

Ignorance and fear are big business

It was suggested I attach a disclaimer to such radical views about freedom, truth and justice. My reply was 'teachers are revolutionaries', as is the education process itself. It got me thinking about how many 'disclaimers' we may be living by without realising it. Maybe instead of rushing to issue disclaimers to truths that others may find offensive we should take a moment to issue a few 'reclaimers' to remind ourselves what we actually stand for and believe in. Everyone has a right to their opinion, but the value of that opinion is usually defined by the knowledge and understanding, the life experience that helped form it. By the same token everyone has the right to be offended by that opinion, but being offended doesn't automatically mean you are right. While I take full responsibility for my thoughts and beliefs, I have no control over what's going on inside your head, how you think or what you believe I am saying. As a teacher it's my job to get the student to use their brain and think for themselves, but not what to think. That's their part in the teacher student relationship.

The first thing I'm sure of is that I'm not sure of anything, and acutely aware of how little I know. Education and the personal development it can bring is about accepting and letting go in equal measure, accepting the new in the form of knowledge and understanding and releasing or letting go of that which we have outgrown, no longer believe in, or no longer reflects the person we have become. Knowledge and understanding is both incremental and incidental, it never comes to us complete. It's a process that's responsive to our desire to find answers to our questions and seek out the truth whatever and where ever it may be. A closed mind is unaware of its own ignorance and can see no further than the limitations of its own rigid beliefs. What I believe to be true is based on my experiences up to this point in time and I readily accept that just because it's what I believe doesn't make it right, and some or all of these beliefs may have to change as I struggle to know myself.

No matter how different we think we are, we are not. The things we have in common, the things that unite us far out way any obvious superficial differences like faith or the colour of our skin. Separateness is a state of mind that if left unchecked leads to alienation and the setting up of borders and boundaries which like the beliefs that created them must be defended at all costs. We mark our territory and say 'this is mine' and what we own gives us a sense of personal worth and identity. Having got it we fear losing it or having someone else take it away from us, so fear becomes our constant companion, on guard watching for some imaginary adversary. Unfortunately we live in a time where ignorance and fear are big business. Governments preach the word of peace while making billions selling arms to third world countries and dictatorships in the name of freedom, In exchange for mineral rights and political influence and power. As ever religion takes the moral high ground; does nothing too radical or confrontational so ensuring the status quo between politics and religion is maintained. 'Gods will' is their mantra; ensuring difficult questions go unanswered; and the buck never stops with the church officials.

World peace is a beautiful aspiration, but there is no profit to be made in peace, and while we place financial gain, political and religious power above the suffering of those deemed worthless and expendable it can never become a reality. Until enlightenment allows those barriers to be dismantled necessity requires brave men and women to stand guard in watch towers the world over so we may sleep soundly at night. They protect a freedom others earned with their lives, freedom, a luxury we take for granted without ever stopping to think of the high price that was paid for our complacency. In a moment of reflection our conscience pricked we find solace in a donation on Remembrance Sunday wearing our Poppy with pride at our financial sacrifice and commitment to a worthy cause, and a contribution to Children in Need buys us peace of mind for at least another year.

The democracy fought for is held in the highest esteem by those who value freedom of speech yet the political system that extols its virtue is so corrupt that no matter whom you vote into office its always 'business as usual'. We are conditioned to believe we have the power to bring about change through the ballot box, but if this were true and our vote had the power to threaten the power brokers behind the politicians, the system would simply be changed in the name of progress in order to redress the balance in their favour. Politics is all about power; and as such is based on lies and deceit; politicians will say and do whatever is necessary to get into a position of power. Once in office they will do whatever they have to, to stay there. To the career politician in it for the long haul democracy is overrated, the electorate is a necessary evil whose voice should be paid lip service to, but only listened to when it's expedient and in the politician's best interest. Not all politicians are corrupt but their influence is limited when the system is corrupt. A lone voice will eventually fall silent as its message falls on deaf ears.

We live in a country whose empire was built on the strength and power of the class system. Although we no longer have an empire the class system and its elitist mindset is as strong as ever and is the foundation upon which the establishment sits. Whatever form of sovereignty it takes, be it constitutional political, financial or religious has one primary objective which is to perpetuate its own existence. This it does through the exercise of power and control in every aspect of our lives. We may believe that we have a choice in everything we do, but if those in positions of authority create and control the options available to us, the power to choose is nothing more than a token gesture given to appease and keep the peace. Every aspect of our lives is controlled, stimulated and regulated. The type of education available to us; the affect this has in the work we are able and qualified to do and the income we have to spend.

Where we live, where we shop and what we buy in those shops are all influenced by decisions made by others on our behalf. The news we see on TV and read about in the press may appear current and topical but the media is governed and controlled by the establishment, and we see what those behind the scenes want us to see. Live TV is still edited and what we see is decided by editors, producers and directors. We may have control of our TV remote but through the power of the media others are able to control to a large extent what we see, think and believe to be true and factual.

Reality TV is a joke in more ways than one, and unfortunately the joke is on us. Regardless of race colour or creed we all share the need to be loved, cared for and appreciated, but there is no profit to be made or power to be gained in global unity. Politics religion and finance dictate that divide, conquer and control is the order of the day, and our ignorance and fear is used against us. To the politicians and power brokers global unity in the form of an enlightened, educated and knowledgeable brotherhood of mankind would be the end of the world as they know it.

Our ignorance and fear is big business and it's this which allows the world order to be as it is. But how do we change what appears at first to be insurmountable. Strength contains its own weakness; every force has within it the seed of its own destruction, and when ignorance is the chosen method of control education, knowledge and understanding becomes the key to its undoing. This is a revolution of awareness that can't be brought about through the use of violence. If violence is the way of the world then we must choose a different path to reach the goal we desire. If we want something different then we must do something different. If we use violence on the pretext of some higher good then we are no better than the rest.

To change a person or to change the world the principle is exactly the same. Change begins with a simple but powerful thought. The desire to gain true knowledge and understanding and with it the power and ability to think for oneself is the nemesis to those who would keep us in the darkness of ignorance and fear. A single thought has the power and potential to change anyone it touches and the transformation begins in the mind that awakens to the reality of what they see before them.

We have a responsibility to think for ourselves, to open our hearts and our minds and to seek out the truth where ever it may be. With knowledge and understanding comes the desire to be heard and to speak not just for ourselves but for those still struggling to find their own voice.

I belong to a human race with brothers and sisters all over this tiny little planet we inhabit. I don't care about the colour of a person's skin, their race religion, or sexual orientation, what matters to me is how they treat others and themselves. I want to live in peace with my fellow man and try to make the world a better place to live, now and for generations to come. This can only be achieved one step at a time and one person at a time. As a student looking to educate myself I hope that my actions create ripples of consciousness that travel out far beyond my own horizons. As a teacher I hope my work stimulates and resonates with another to such an extent a life changing thought is born in a mind that has just awoken.

Chapter Seventy-One

Forever present in the past

In silent prayer I seek guidance; in silent meditation I listen for the answers that would take me to a place of knowledge and understanding where the past, present and future are one. Here translucent lines of time merge as the past present and future disappear before my eyes and time stands still. Images fade only to return like distant echo's to be swept beyond my grasp as I try to hold on to precious memories worn and warmed by the passing of time.

Sights and sounds play across a sea of emotion that ebb and flow with each new vision. Sounds long past evoke a life long forgotten, before age had taken its time from me. Voices that once brought comfort are no more than whispers in a breeze carried away like opportunities lost. Once again I'm alone with only my thoughts for comfort. Like a child looking at its own reflection, I stare in wonderment; but the face I see before me is not my own. I see shadows of what was, what is and all that shall be. With a gentleness born of innocence I reach out only to see the images dissolve and trickle through my fingers like grains of sand. All that once was, is no more; all that is, is but a memory of what is yet to come. What I thought would stand as testament will eventually be lost to memory as life moves on and covers them with the dust of new experiences. Built by the hands of man, all must one day succumb to the hands of time.

Stillness descends as silently as night falls, and peace prevails; before me I am shown the legacy of love bequeathed as a consequence of my actions. Love and kindness; ripples spreading far beyond my own horizon to gently rest on distant shores. Infinity lies beyond the limits of my understanding; yet my capacity to love and be loved allows me to transcend time and guide and support the faltering footsteps of those yet to be born. The seeds of my good deeds sown in the knowledge and understanding they will one day bear fruit as a testament to my passing.

Chapter Seventy-Two

Am I there yet?

We are led to believe that the act of 'trying' is a necessary and inescapable part of any achievement, to 'try' is to attempt and to 'do' is to succeed. We believe that trying is normal; it's a part of normal everyday life. Yet what we believe to be normal is nothing more than a personal or subjective point of view. As we know your point of view or more precisely your view point is determined by where you are at any given time. What is considered 'normal' by one person may appear totally strange to another. The act of trying contains an element of uncertainty, when we say we will try we are unsure of whether we will succeed or fail in our attempt. We automatically link trying to a judgement or a measurement of personal ability, and in trying we may in some way fail.

We find it easier to say I will try than I will do. Part of the problem with trying and doing is our desire to judge everything we do from a 'better than' or 'not as good as' point of view. We convince ourselves before we have even attempted something, we can't do it we can only try. We then judge our efforts against some unrealistic goal and find our efforts lacking as we fail to measure up to the ideal Do we need to try? Is it possible to 'just do' without sitting in judgement all the time? What would happen if we replaced trying with simply doing, would we achieve more, would we be less judgemental of others and ourselves? To try is to attempt, to do is to complete, yet in reality all action is complete as it should be the moment it is carried out. It's only our desire to judge and criticise that makes it appear less than it actually is. Doing is trying by another name; doing is achievement without judgement, criticism, or guilt. Creation is a process; it's never finite, it's a gradual conscious evolution that involves thought, attention, intention, and action, 'doing' is creation by another name. Our consciousness is both attention and intention; our attention energises and our intention transforms what we focus upon, our attention is concerned with the present while our intention creates the future we desire, or not as the case may be. Doing is intention by another name.

The artist doesn't sketch the first line onto the canvas then step back and say 'It's ok, but it's not a very good portrait'. The writer doesn't put pen to paper and number the first page then sit back and say 'It's ok but it's not a novel'. The builder doesn't lay the first foundation stone then berate his own efforts because it doesn't match up with the architects design.

When we say that we can't write, draw, or do anything we are making judgements on our own abilities based comparisons made against someone or something that we believe to be better than us. Doing has nothing to do with ability or the lack of it, we all have the ability to do and enjoy the experience without the need to judge our actions from a better or worse point of view. Isn't it better to say 'I haven't learnt how to do that yet, but I will do it'? The difference between those who try and those who do is one of judgement and belief. Those who see their actions no matter how small as necessary and complete keep their attention on the details while focusing their intention on the end result.

We learn by doing; and we do what we come to know and understand. Doing is a statement of attention and intention, and recognises that every action no matter how small and seemingly insignificant is complete and a success in itself. Not to be judged prematurely against some unrealistic ideal or belief. Chinese philosopher Lao Tzu once said 'A journey of a thousand miles begins with a single step' how foolish it would be for a traveller to take their first step then ask 'am I there yet'?

Chapter Seventy-Three

Guilt is the Superglue of our emotions

The secret to letting go of stuff is to stop feeling guilty about the mistakes you have made. You may think good people have a duty to feel guilty but you would be wrong. Guilt is a choice not an obligation and as long as we feel and fear guilt we will remain attached to the very stuff we need to let go off. But we have a duty to feel guilty for our past mistakes don't we? No we don't. Our duty is to educate ourselves so that we can recognise where we went wrong. To have the maturity to look beyond our actions and consider the reasons and circumstances for the choices made, and where possible make amends.

Did we lack knowledge and understanding which in itself reduces the number of choices available to us, or did we simply not consider or foresee the consequences of our actions. With this awareness comes the realisation we hold within ourselves the power to create a better future if we would only let go of the guilt we have attached to the past. Mistakes do not make a bad person; they make us fallible and human capable of making wrong decisions that can with clarity, be changed and put right. Regret is the seed from which knowledge and understanding grows and change becomes the fruit of our labours. We do what we do until we know better, then comes the duty and responsibility to do better. Part of that duty is to forgive ourselves for mistakes real or imaginary, to cut ourselves some slack, and to accept that critical judgement no matter how righteous it may first appear, has no place in the healing process which seeks to unite not divide.

To heal is to rejoin that which has become broken and separated so that we may be made whole in mind, body and spirit. We begin to heal when we begin forgive ourselves and we help others to heal when we release the ties that bind us. Guilt doesn't heal nor instigate change; knowledge and understanding does. We change when we realise that change is not only possible it's fundamental part of spiritual and personal growth and of life itself. We change when we accept we have the power and ability to change no matter how afraid we may feel whilst in the grip of ignorance and fear. Faith, superstition or the need to feel loved and valued are no substitute for knowledge and understanding. Misplaced devotion or loyalty to a person or belief system can lead us to sacrifice our happiness, self-respect, health, and wellbeing. The ability to think for ourselves brings with it a desire to be heard and to let go of all limiting beliefs and relationships that are destructive and corrosive to our health and quality of life.

Guilt would keep us attached using emotional blackmail implying a duty of care to others overrides our own needs and the desire to think of one self is selfish and shows a weakness in character and personal values. Ignorance and fear covers a multitude of sins and has many faces. Sometimes the ones we need to let go of are those guilt says we should hang onto the most. If attachment robs us of our peace of mind, our health and happiness, it is poison to the soul and poison is still poison no matter what form it takes or how lovingly crafted it appears.

To those who would control us forgiveness of self is an act of clemency that is above and beyond our personal authority to grant. We are conditioned to believe only a higher power in this life, or the next can forgive us for our sins and absolve us of our guilt. Our ignorance and fear are used against us to such an extent we come to believe to forgive ourselves is a sin in itself

375

requiring even greater punishment for daring to release ourselves from the burden of guilt.

Guilt like fear hides in the shadows of our mind and have no power other than that which we give then. Both use our ignorance to create the illusion of power, elevate their position of importance and justify their existence. The nemesis of ignorance and fear is knowledge and understanding. It sees them for what they are and knows what fear asks us to hold onto the tightest is what we need to let go of the most. In doing so we come to realise that what keeps us captive is nothing more than our own debilitating belief. In ignorance we have taken on the role of judge and jury and found ourselves guilty requiring punishment, in many cases we suffer a life sentence of self inflicted torture denied pardon or parole. As jailor we hold the key to our release and with it comes responsibility for we alone can use to set ourselves free. Freedom granted; unlocking the door we step into the light. The fear faced evaporates and the fall from grace is an illusion that allows our spirit to soar as the burden of guilt is finally let go of and set aside.

Chapter Seventy-Four

Make peace with your past so you can part on good terms

When circumstances can't be changed the way we look at the situation provides the key to our release from the past, and our ability and willingness to move forward. If we view change in life as the only constant we must accept it as part of our evolutionary process. Development on the other hand can be both revolutionary and liberating as it requires us to change our perspective and begin to let go of the things that no longer serve us by accepting what was; what is and most importantly what can be. When we judge a situation we attach ourselves to the event and become defined as much by the feelings and emotions that judgement creates as by the events themselves. Acceptance does not mean we condone or free others from the consequences of their actions; rather acceptance is a part of the self-healing process of forgiveness and the first step in securing our own freedom.

No matter what circumstances dictate we retain absolute control over our attitude, and how we look at a situation will determine how we feel about it and how much control it has over us. Negative emotions such as fear anger and guilt are self imposed judgement and limitations, and no matter how justifiable, bind us to the situation and people who helped create them.

Time and distance can be great healers; perspective comes to us in the lessons we learn and brings clarity through a growing knowledge and understanding of oneself. As negative emotions bind us so positive ones can help us re-evaluate who we are, and release those thoughts, feelings and emotions that keep us trapped. We cannot change the past, what is done is done and no amount of regret can ever change that. As long as we provide a sanctuary for fear anger and guilt in our lives time and distance can offer no protection from the punishment we inflict upon ourselves by revisiting painful memories and opening old wounds.

When we accept what was, what is and what can be we come to realise that the past no matter how painful was instrumental in the making of the person we have become. Battered and bruised maybe, but it's those challenges that helped change us, and forged within us the will and determination to survive, overcome and make a difference in life. The past is as much a part of us as is the present and our future. Making peace with our past first requires us to make peace with ourselves by accepting, loving and forgiving ourselves unconditionally free from the limitations of judgement. Once we are able to do so time and distance can begin to finally heal old wounds, and with the learning knowledge and understanding brings we can be grateful for the lessons the past has provided, offer our thanks and part on good terms.

Chapter Seventy-Five

The nature of abuse

Knowledge and understanding never comes to us complete and neither does the ignorance and fear that allows abuse in all of its many forms to happen. The abuse we initially experience is never the complete article or the finished product that can have such catastrophic effects on people's lives. Abuse is incremental, it develops and grows in relation to the freedom it enjoys and its ability to express itself free from resistance or constrains that would hold it in check. The bully in the playground, the domineering parent the controlling partner, or the manipulative carer, the practice of abuse may be different but the underlying principle remains the same. When the thought and the belief abuse is a legitimate means of gaining and maintaining power and control is acted upon it becomes the reality. Once the initial thought and belief are accepted as the norm, justification for those actions becomes easier as the level of abuse escalates in order to maintain a level of control, disempowering the person being abused in order to feed the addiction of abuse.

The bullies in the playground and the abusive partner or parent are simply points on the same scale separated only by position, opportunity and power available to them to vent their own inadequacies. In the absence of knowledge and understanding ignorance and fear will always take control, and those who stand by and remain silent are guilty by association. When circumstances provide us with comfort and safety from such abuse, complacency can become our sedative of choice.

Detachment frees us from the need to feel guilty or accept any personal responsibility It allows us to turn away, for out of sight is out of mind. A global solution begins as a personal responsibility not to change others but to first and foremost change ourselves, our perceptions of what is acceptable and gain a better understanding of the insidious nature of abuse. An internal desire to learn must become an external experience; a change in perception is a prerequisite to bring about the changes we wish to experience. Healing of any description is impossible without knowledge and understanding and those who invest heavily in abuse do so to appease their own feelings of inadequacy. They recognise the need to disempower, create a sense of hopelessness and a false mindset of ignorance and fear. Knowledge and understanding is the nemesis of all forms of abuse and the ultimate undoing of all abusers, for they know instinctively their power lies in the suppression of the mind, body and spirit. Of these, the mind becomes a prison and the hardest to break free from. The place where all abuse begins and ultimately where it must end.

Chapter Seventy-Six

Reclaiming your personal power

Anyone who has ever been used abused or victimised will know what it's like to feel powerless. That cold and desolate place of fear and self loathing we learn to live with and come to accept as our own. When powerlessness is 'learned' as opposed to institutionalised and imposed powerlessness, it becomes second nature and takes on a life of its own. An abused child will more often than not grow up to feel powerless as an adult, even if those who took their power from them are no longer alive, or a part of their lives. This early negative conditioning forms a mental and emotional blueprint we look to replicate in other aspects of our lives. In doing so we may replace one abusive role model for another. The abusive parent is replaced by the domineering partner, husband or wife who finds themselves promoted to a position of power and authority. Without realising it we sometimes become our own worst enemy. We must take great care when the abuser has done with us, we don't continue where they have left off. We can do this by keeping oneself locked into forms of self-abuse or harmful compulsive behaviour. Our thoughts become toxic and through them our psychology becomes our biology and the powerlessness is internalised. To reclaim that personal power we must first understand the processes involved so they become meaningful and more than a loose fitting casual concept. We need to understand what the different elements look like before we can search for them.

In every situation there is something for us to know before there is something to do, it's this increase in knowledge and understanding that is the first step in any healing process. The first tentative steps in reclaiming our personal power begin with the healing of oneself. Healing your self is the ultimate demonstration of your personal power and control. Healing is education by another name and if we want to reclaim our personal power then we must educate ourselves first and foremost. All users and abusers know instinctively or intellectually that knowledge is power and the key to freedom.

It's in their best interest to keep us locked in the darkness created by ignorance and fear. Knowledge and understanding brings the light of clarity by which we are able to see much of their perceived power is illusionary made real by our belief in their dominance and our vulnerability.

We all have legitimate entitlements that are formulated by our human rights. We have the right to live a life free from physical, mental emotional and sexual abuse. And while these can be considered our birthright they still need to be understood, valued and at times defended against those who would deny us the freedom they bring. We have the right to be treated with respect and to express ourselves freely and most importantly, we have the right to ask for what we need and to defend that right should it be unfairly withheld or maliciously denied. Our voice and our ability to speak up for ourselves is an outward expression of our personal power. Unfortunately when we are robbed of this power we can lose our ability to speak out against the injustice that we face. Finding an alternative means of expression through the development of a new skill and ability can lead to the rediscovery of our voice and with it the courage and ability to speak our own truth. Success can have a very liberating effect and help us find the confidence to stand on our own feet and seek rightful recognition for who we are and what we believe in.

The sting of another's inconsideration is painful enough, but when the abuse is deliberate and sustained the pain and resulting trauma can last a lifetime. Sometimes the damage is so great that professional help is required before any form of personal development can be even be considered and put into place. If we need help then we must ensure that we get it. No matter what form that help takes it must initiate the empowering process whereby we feel able to take the first tentative steps in reclaiming ownership for our life 'one right' at a time. If we slavishly believe that others have the power to set us free we will remain trapped in a prison of our own making. Relying on faith, hope or the charity of others as our saviour is misplaced and does us the greatest dis-service. It works on the premise that others alone have the power to free us from feeling powerless thus creating a self defeating vicious circle. Actively seeking advice and guidance is not the same as passively sitting back and waiting for someone else to tell us how to live our lives. We must ultimately take responsibility for our education, healing and personal development.

Reclaiming personal power requires a change to take place and begins with a healing of the self. This is only possible when knowledge and understanding is present for healing of any description is impossible without it. To achieve this we need to change our focus. Instead of looking to others for praise, permission or validation we need to look inward, because that's where we will find the answers we are looking for.

Healing of the self begins the moment knowledge and understanding becomes a greater reality than the ignorance and fear that appears to be in control of our life. When we begin to heal ourselves we have begun our journey towards the reclamation of our personal power. Our thoughts can be toxic, but by the same token they can also be the most up lifting and life fulfilling resource at our disposal. This reclamation is an incremental transition because knowledge and understanding never comes to us complete. Each step leads to the next; success builds upon success thus providing us with a solid foundation built on.

Personal power is made up of many components; self-respect, self-worth, trust, courage, strength, love, and compassion. These elements are reflective of the individual's needs and personal circumstances they may face. Each has to be worked at to be secured before it can be put into place. Often the most difficult element to reclaim is the power of forgiveness. Primarily the forgiveness of self for being a victim and for any guilt or misplaced responsibility we may feel. We must also reclaim the power and ability to forgive others. To forgive is not about condoning what they did or freeing them from responsibility. We forgive so that we are released from the control over us, and more importantly the consequences of their actions. Although the feeling of powerless creates a void in our life it never leaves us completely empty. It leaves a residue of negativity; what we give up, or have taken away from us is replaced with anger guilt, frustration anxiety and self loathing. Much of which is hidden, and we must come to recognise, accept and release these feelings, emotions and beliefs before we can begin to heal. With the lack of power comes the shadow of hopelessness and despair and the belief that the situation is permanent and beyond repair. Those who use, abuse and victimise us help cultivate these feelings of isolation to satisfy their own needs, feed into their own sense of inadequacy and maintain their control.

To reclaim our personal power we must first become aware of the fact that we have either given it away to others or it has been taken away from us by those with the strength, position, power and authority to do so. We must then be willing to accept that our power can be reclaimed and with help and guidance make changes in our thoughts, beliefs and actions to create this necessary transition. A major part of this personal reclamation is the act of letting go. This apparent contradiction is a powerful step in the process. The letting go of debilitating beliefs creates the space in our hearts and minds for personal power to return home, become established and grow into a new reality.

Once we have reclaimed our personal power we have to ensure that we don't become complacent and slip back into the old way of doing things at the expense of our health and wellbeing. If we do it's important that we don't consider this a failure, better we view it as a lesson that needed to be revisited, a period of revision so that the lesson learnt stays fresh and at the forefront of our mind. Reclaiming our personal power is the short term goal. Safeguarding it and ensuring we never knowingly or willingly give it away to another has to be our long term objective for the sake of our health, happiness and peace of mind. The healing of self is the ultimate expression of personal power and self-love. When knowledge and understanding educates us to this fact we will discover that still quiet voice within that says 'I can do this'.

Chapter Seventy-Seven

Judgement of others is a luxury we can't afford

We don't use Reiki to change people, or to make them a better person. We use it to help the person change themselves if they choose to do so. To give freely is to give without restrictions or conditions. To give in the knowledge they will receive what they need, not what we think they should have, or to bring about the changes we think are necessary they in order to be a "good person" deserving of Reiki, or our time and energy. The only person we are responsible for changing is ourselves and until we are ready, willing and able to do so, we have no right to sit in judgement on another person's life choices or their progress. Judgement is a luxury we can't afford for it highlights our own personal development needs attention.

Our desire and commitment to give Reiki to someone we like should be exactly the same to those we dislike. If not our ego is sitting in judgement and deciding who, gets what and why, and we should never sit in judgement of someone who sins differently to us. Once we let go of judgement our job is done. We trust Reiki to do what only it can do, and accept the person will receive what they need. From that point on, it's down to them.

Chapter Seventy-Eight

The spiritual concept of not giving a shit

If you learn not to give a shit you will definitely be a lot happier. I can't promise you will live longer but you will definitely be a lot happier with life and in yourself. The problem people have with not giving a shit is the misconception of what it actually means. They mistakenly think if you don't give a shit you don't care. This couldn't be further from the truth and is the total opposite to the development of the spiritual attitude of not giving a shit. I don't give a shit about so many things, and the list is getting longer day by day, as I become more aware of the healing not giving a shit manifests into my life.

Do I care about things? Yes absolutely. I care passionately about many things. The strange thing is, the less bullshit I allow in my life, and not giving a shit about the things that aren't important and don't require a reaction or my energy, the greater the passion and energy I find within myself for the truly important things in life. Not giving a shit is a spiritual practice and when applied diligently it has the power to help transform our lives and help cultivate meaningful things we feel passionate about.

How much misplaced guilt, poor self-worth and low self-esteem hide behind the shit we stress about. Take a moment to check out your emotional and mental baggage you are carrying. The labels will be negative. There are no weight restrictions to this hand luggage you can carry as much as you want as long as you want, even if it kills you.

The good thing is you can put it down whenever you want. It's your journey and your baggage, all you have to do is decide you don't need this shit anymore and then let it go.

Earth Angel

Brought into this world to develop and grow; I hope as I have struggled to find the truth I have made the way a little easier for others, and given them hope in their darkest moments. May my time here make a difference to the world, and my work help those who will follow in our footsteps? With all my heart, and with all I have learnt, I hope I have given as much to the world as I have taken, and one day leave it a better place for my being here.

I pray that I have learnt enough to love without regret, forgive without hesitation, and to never keep account of my own good deeds or another person's failings

Our time here is short and as I use precious moments to look back on what I have achieved in this life, please don't let my last thoughts be "Shit, I cocked that up". For all of the things I have done and shouldn't have done, for all of the things I shouldn't have said, for all of the things I have left undone I ask your forgiveness.

When my time comes to return home, let the love I have shown fill the space I leave behind and my memory fill hearts with joy and laughter of those who care to remember me. My friends walk softly, speak kindly and above all, gentle with yourself. Try to remember who you are, for in that moment you bring light into the world.

Final Thought for Your Consideration and Future Success

The mind - body connection

Being positive is a wonderful thing but you also have to be realistic. You find the great spiritual teachers were positive in their outlook but also grounded in their attitude to life. They advocated positive change but they also recognised the realities of everyday life that made those changes necessary. They may have taught about raising awareness, but their feet were very firmly on the ground for they understood to change any situation you must first accept it for what it is. Reality can be harsh and unyielding and we can be tempted to retreat into a world of make believe. But illusion lacks real substance and offers cold comfort when having to face the challenges life presents us with.

Fearing failure or lacking belief in our own ability we go for the safe option. We do what we really don't want to do in the mistaken belief that we are in some way stacking the odds of success in our favour.

Unfortunately, life has a habit of throwing us a curve ball and the best laid plans can go ''tits up'' when we least expect it. If we live in the land of make believe we can ensure life is perfect, but real life is made up of highs and lows, successes and failures which provide purpose, meaning and value to the life we lead. We have to make choices on a daily basis and hopefully those choices are considered and informed but fear can disempower even the most positive person and trick them into playing it safe.

It's inevitable that we will at some time fail in life. But surely it's better that we try and fail doing something we feel inspired to do, rather than settle for an easier option that may satisfy our physical needs but starves our spirit, and leads to an empty unfulfilled life.

Spiritual Journey

Hand in hand I walk with the child within, looking at the world with eyes of wonder and joy. With love and compassion we view all things, without judgment or attachment, innocence born of wisdom. We are one with each other on a journey to discover our spirituality.

Standing upon high, amidst the raging storm, arms outstretched, our faces turned towards the heavens we feel the rush of spirit, yet within a place of peace and tranquility for we are one with the universe.

A forest clearing standing in silent homage, to the power of the earth that brings forth all life. Alive to that moment when our senses are attuned to the love that surrounds us and time stands still. We walk in green pastures that calm the mind and soothe the troubled heart.

We gaze into still water that reflects the tranquility of the soul at peace with itself. Our beating hearts intrude upon the silence, a rhythm in tune with the power that pulsates around us and we are at one with the spirit of nature.

About the Author

A Reiki practitioner since 1999, Phillip started teaching Reiki in 2000 and using those skills and abilities he has spent the majority of the last seventeen years working with a wide range of social and educational needs including Autism and ADHD. Working with addicts dependent on alcohol and drugs, people whose lives were extremely violent and abusive, and others who had to deal with severe mental health issues. This has enabled Phillip to work extensively in the private sector, schools, colleges, education and care in the community, the prison service and psychiatric units. In 2016 he decided to semi retire from full time employment to concentrate on developing his career as a published author and the setting up of his Reiki personal development programme at the Chilton Community College. Phillip is the author of "Reiki Hold my beer, I've got this! " book.

Made in the USA
Middletown, DE
09 January 2019